The Legacy
of Reinhold Niebuhr

Photograph by Phillipe Halsman—used with his permission

REINHOLD NIEBUHR
(1892—1971)

The Legacy
of Reinhold Niebuhr

Edited by NATHAN A. SCOTT, JR.

The University of Chicago Press
Chicago and London

This work also appeared as volume 54, number 4 (October 1974), of
The Journal of Religion, under the editorship of Nathan A. Scott, Jr.,
B. A. Gerrish, and David Tracy and published by The University of
Chicago Press.

The University of Chicago Press, Chicago 60637
The University of Chicago Press, Ltd., London

International Standard Book Number: 0-226-74297-0
Library of Congress Catalog Card Number: 74-30714

To
Ursula M. Niebuhr

Nothing that is worth doing can be achieved in our lifetime; therefore we must be saved by hope. Nothing which is true or beautiful or good makes complete sense in any immediate context of history; therefore we must be saved by faith. Nothing we do, however virtuous, can be accomplished alone; therefore we must be saved by love. No virtuous act is quite as virtuous from the standpoint of our friend or foe as it is from our standpoint; therefore we must be saved by the final form of love which is forgiveness. [REINHOLD NIEBUHR, *The Irony of American History* (New York: Charles Scribner's Sons, 1952), p. 63]

Contents

Introduction

Nathan A. Scott, Jr.

Though illness over a long period prior to his death in the spring of 1971 had perforce greatly limited the degree of his involvement in the major forums of recent years, the pressure of Reinhold Niebuhr's legacy is widely felt today as that of a towering figure in American intellectual life of the past half-century. That this should be so may seem a little strange, for he was not a man of letters, or a philosopher, or an historian, or a scientist—or a practitioner of any of those cultural disciplines that carry the largest prestige in our time: on the contrary, he was by profession a Christian theologian, and his career was thus claimed by commitments than which there are perhaps none less likely to be deemed commendable by those whom Friedrich Schleiermacher named "the cultured despisers of religion." Yet is was amongst this very numerous constituency that Niebuhr was accorded an esteem quite as notable as that wherewith he was regarded in the theological community itself, so much so indeed that the philosopher Morton White once envisaged the prospect of an alliance of Atheists for Niebuhr. Apart from the German *émigré* Paul Tillich, long his colleague on the faculty of Union Theological Seminary, there is in fact no other theologian of this century—not even excepting such distinguished Europeans as Karl Barth and Rudolf Bultmann—whose impact has struck so deeply into the mind of the age: by their own testimony, so diverse and representative a group of his contemporaries as the critic F. O. Matthiessen, the diplomat George Kennan, the poet W. H. Auden, the Jewish theologian Abraham Heschel, the political theorist Hans Morgenthau, the psychiatrist Robert Coles, the historian Arthur Schlesinger, Jr., and the great martyr of the Negro freedom movement, Martin Luther King, found in him (as have countless others of equal distinction who might be cited) a vision of the human endeavor—of the hazard with which it is fraught and the high promise its sober sustainment may hold forth—that was profoundly quickening. Even for many who are in no way prepared to give their own suffrage to a religious position, the astonishing brilliance of Niebuhr's dialectic has often had the effect of wonderfully clarifying their sense of the complication and peril that are a part of the human horizon. And thus he, more so perhaps than any other thinker of the recent past, is felt to have invested the great themes of Christian theology with a strange kind of relevance to the political and intellectual ferment of the modern period.

*   *   *

Reinhold Niebuhr was born in Wright City, Missouri, in the summer of 1892, but the scene of his formative years was the little town of Lincoln, Illinois, where his father, Gustav Niebuhr, was pastor to the local congregation of the Evangelical Synod (a small Lutheran denomination which merged with a Calvinist communion in 1934 to form the Evangelical and Reformed Church, this in turn merging with the Congregationalists in 1956 to form the United Church of Christ). The elder Niebuhr, who had come to this country from Germany in late adolescence, was a man of limited but of sound and solid learning, and one who kept a large admiration for those American public men—like Lincoln and Theodore Roosevelt and Carl Schurz—who struck him as exemplifying the liberality and benevolence marking the national spirit at its best. So, given his intellectual culture and the breadth of his political sympathies, it is not surprising that, in this conservative little prairie community of prosperous German-American farmers, his son Reinhold should have regarded him as "the most interesting man in . . . town"[1]and should have chosen (along with his brother H. Richard Niebuhr, later himself also to achieve high prominence as a theologian) to follow him in the Christian ministry.

After completing his secondary education in Lincoln and after four years at Elmhurst College (in Elmhurst, Illinois), Reinhold then undertook his divinity studies at Eden Theological Seminary in a suburban district of Saint Louis, where he received the Bachelor of Divinity degree in 1913. Two further years at Yale followed, and, in the autumn of 1915, after having received an M.A. in New Haven the previous spring, he took up his first major assignment, as the minister of the Bethel Evangelical Church in Detroit. Here it was, as the pastor of a small parish unconnected with the more fashionable precincts of this ample Midwestern city, that he had his first experience of a modern industrial metropolis and of the terrible costs its productivity exacted of working-class people, in a period when the lords of American industry had not yet begun to face any significant countervailing force in an effective labor union movement. Detroit was, of course, very largely the creature of the Ford Motor Company, which, as it was daily turning out at huge profit the hundreds of little "tin lizzies" produced on its assembly lines, was loudly trumpeting forth the magnanimity with which its employees were being handled—in the five-day week and the minimum wage of

[1]John Cogley, "An Interview with Reinhold Niebuhr," *McCall's Magazine* 93, no. 5 (February 1966): 171.

five dollars per day that were being offered. But, as this young pastor was soon to discover, the conditions of work in the automobile foundries, as they had been cannily devised by the efficiency experts, left young men so ravaged by their labor that confinement to their beds on Saturdays and Sundays was often a necessary prelude to their returning to the factories on Monday morning. Nor did the Ford and Chevrolet and Chrysler executives, when they congratulated the industry on its munificence toward its workmen, speak of the seasonal shutdowns when, in long periods of retooling necessitated by annual changes in styling, the labor force was laid off without any compensating indemnity. Indeed, the entire structure of the city's social and economic affairs was filled with such ambiguity, and, on every side, this young man found himself confronted by distressing evidences of how precarious may be the situation of the individual person in a technocratic society. So, despite the misgivings felt by some of his more conservative parishioners, he quickly committed himself to full participation in all the more forward-looking movements of civic advance on the local scene. By the mid-1920s his arraignment of bourgeois democracy, of its failure to achieve economic justice and to manage a stable international peace, had propelled him into the circles of Christian pacifism, as it was also preparing him to join the Socialist Party. More importantly perhaps, it was an arraignment regularly finding a platform in such organs of the national intelligence as the *Atlantic Monthly, The Christian Century, The World Tomorrow,* and *The Nation.* And the career began unmistakably to be in full tide with the publication in 1927 of his first book, *Does Civilization Need Religion?*, which, as "A Study in the Social Resources and Limitations of Religion in Modern Life," was a direct outgrowth of his Detroit experience.

In the autumn of 1928 Niebuhr took up residence in New York City as a member of the faculty of Union Theological Seminary, where, despite the many prestigious university chairs that were later to be offered, he chose to remain until his retirement in 1960. Though his removal from the pressures of an urban pastorate to a professorial berth brought new opportunities for systematic research that were to make for a great deepening of his thought, he seems never to have intended, however, that an academic career should foreclose political engagement. He remained a decisive figure in the Fellowship for a Christian Social Order, and, after its absorption in 1928 into the leading pacifist organization of the period, the Fellowship of Reconciliation, he became the Fellowship's national chairman. By 1929, with John Dewey and Paul Douglas, he was sitting on the Executive Committee of the League for Independent Political Action. In 1930 he was the Socialist Party's candidate for Congress in the Morningside Heights community on New York's upper west side. Moreover, in the same year, he was founding the Fellowship of Socialist

Christians. And, throughout the remainder of the decade, despite extensive foreign travel and his broadening activities in the international ecumenical movement among the churches of non-Roman Christendom, he was—through his leadership in numerous political and religious associations, through his lecturing and preaching across the land, and through the torrent of books and essays produced by his restless pen—at the center of all the important debate being called forth on the American scene by the social-economic stoppages of the Depression and by the ever more ominously looming clouds thrown across the horizon by Hitler's Germany.

The kind of liberal Protestant apologetic that he represented when he joined the Union Seminary faculty—an apologetic (as enunciated by his first book) in behalf of the "reverence for human personality" promoted by what he vaguely denominated as "high religion"—was, however, in these years undergoing drastic reassessment. For the social idealism bequeathed him by the theological tradition of Washington Gladden and Walter Rauschenbusch and Shailer Mathews, however generous may have been its vision of mutuality and compassion as the fundamental norms of collective life, did not, as he came to feel, proffer anything like a sufficiently adequate standpoint, since its tendency was to make religion little more than an adornment of conventional morality. Nor did its ardent espousals of the "service motive" strike him as calculated to foster any sober allowance for the very limited degree to which moral suasion may be expected to overcome human egoism or to dislodge exploitative power from its position of advantage. And, furthermore, he was becoming convinced that the central traditions of modern secular liberalism, taken in the terms either of Locke or of Jefferson or of Stuart Mill or of John Dewey, reflected an equal incompetence before the stubborn actualities of social injustice. Here, it was assumed that the root of social disorder lay in some kind of "cultural lag" whose alleviation awaited only a further extension of enlightenment through the broadening of educational opportunity and the application in the public realm of experimental procedures comparable to those employed in the scientific laboratory: thus, as it was often assumed, the "natural harmony" of the human order may be reinstated and sustained.

Increasingly, however, as he looked out upon the disarray of the 1930s, Niebuhr was persuaded that the reconstruction of this broken time must be an affair neither of moral preachment nor of pedagogy but of politics. His own country, along with the entire Western world, had been reduced to a shambles of insolvency and breakdown: millions were unemployed and hungry and without hope: everywhere there was confusion and dismay. And, in the context of these extremities, the moralism of Christian meliorists and the rationalist faith of secular liberalism seemed equally irrelevant, since neither had any firm purchase on what he took to be the central issue—namely, the necessity arising when large numbers of men are the victims of social and economic disinheritance of serious reassessment of the established allocations of power.

Indeed, the writing of his famous book of 1932, *Moral Man and Immoral Society,* was prompted by nothing so much as by his sense of the need then to confront both secular and religious liberalism with the exigent fact of power as the decisive reality in the relations between men. And this he did with an iconoclasm whose bluntness seemed, particularly to many of his theological colleagues, to be (as the English theologian Alan Richardson recalls) "the outpouring of a cynical and perverse spirit, very far removed from the benevolent and sanguine serenity which was held to be the hallmark of a truly Christian mind."[2] Nor was the effect of his "realism" any less abrasive in the secular intellectual community. But, nevertheless, his purpose was to lay down the lesson that, however much "it may be possible . . . to establish just relations between individuals . . . purely by moral and rational suasion," in ". . . inter-group relations this is practically an impossibility. The relations between groups must therefore always be predominantly political rather than ethical, that is, they will be determined by the proportion of power which each group possesses at least as much as by any rational and moral appraisal of the comparative needs and claims of each group."[3] Given, in other words, the incorrigibly self-regarding impulses that control social collectives, decency of life within the general community will be guaranteed not by a more perfect system of education or by a more ethically rigorous religion but only by a system of checks and balances that preserves unto each group a measure of power sufficient to weigh effectively against that of any other group by which it might be maltreated. Which was, of course, for Niebuhr to say that, in the ordering of society, the relevant norm is not love but justice—not the "beloved community" of Protestant liberal idealism or that rational mutuality dreamt of by secular pedagogues and moralists, but the equitable distribution of power within the body politic.

It was such an account of the political order that *Moral Man and Immoral Society* rendered, and a similar stringency marked the argument of the book that followed it two years later, *Reflections on the End of an Era,* in which Niebuhr's insistence again was on the necessity of a political theory radical "not only in the realistic nature of its analysis but [also] in its willingness to challenge the injustices of a given social system by

---

[2] Alan Richardson, "Reinhold Niebuhr as Apologist," in *Reinhold Niebuhr: His Religious, Social, and Political Thought,* ed. Charles W. Kegley and Robert W. Bretall (New York: Macmillan Co., 1956), p. 218.

[3] Reinhold Niebuhr, *Moral Man and Immoral Society: A Study in Ethics and Politics* (New York: Charles Scribner's Sons, 1932), pp. xxii–xxiii.

setting power against power until a more balanced equilibrium of power is achieved."[4] The book of 1934 belongs, indeed, to the period in which he was inclined to think of himself as a "Christian Marxist." But, though his frequent chafing over what he conceived to be the aimlessness of the Roosevelt administration in the early 'thirties did for a time issue in some scepticism about the capacity of capitalism to rectify its own malaise, his allegiance to Marxism never ran very deep. Its emphasis on the organic nature of society, its view of class conflict as the seat of social dynamism, its special kind of agnosticism with respect to social ideology, its sense of economic inequality as the essence of social injustice—all this he found to be exceedingly suggestive. Yet he never harbored any illusions about the demonry that, already in the early 'thirties, appeared to him to be the expectable consequence of the fanatical Messianism engendered by the Communist movement. So early, indeed, as the spring of 1931 he was declaring that "only a sentimentalist could be oblivious of the possibilities of Napoleonic ventures in the forces which are seething in Russia."[5] And, as the decade drew to a close, the Moscow trials of 1938 and the Hitler-Stalin pact of 1939 brought what he, along with many others, took to be unignorable evidence of the unconscionableness of the Soviet oligarchy. But, for a brief period, the rhetoric of Marxism did present itself as a kind of reinforcement of his critique of liberal moralism; and it is this stage in his thought which is represented by *Reflections on the End of an Era*.

Given his deepening conviction that social responsibility could be exercised only by way of a sober reckoning with the calculus of political and economic power, it was, of course, inevitable that his relations with the pacifist movement should become strained; and, indeed, in January 1934, he announced his departure from the Fellowship of Reconciliation.[6] His pacifist friends persisted in their disconsolate reveries about the happy transformations of the world that would be possible "if only" men would follow the "way of Jesus" and the "way of the Cross," and their wistfulness, as Niebuhr had come to feel, was merely an indication of how inadequately their sentimental perfectionism prepared them to deal with the concrete realities of politics. They conceived the peace of the Kingdom of God to be a simple historical possibility and thought the ethic of *agape* proposed by the Sermon on the Mount yields a proximate stratagem of action—"the politics of love"—relevant to social exigencies. But, in the event, this stratagem entailed nothing other

[4]Reinhold Niebuhr, *Reflections on the End of an Era* (New York: Charles Scribner's Sons, 1934), p. 230.

[5]Reinhold Niebuhr, "The Religion of Communism," *Atlantic Monthly* 147 (April 1931): 465.

[6]See Reinhold Niebuhr, "Why I Leave the F.O.R.," *Christian Century*, January 3, 1934, pp. 17-19.

than "non-participation" in conflict—which, as Niebuhr finally concluded, is but a fastidious abdication from the field of responsibility, and one which, when it offers itself as a serious political alternative, must be adjudged utterly fatuous. For the great continuing problem of collective life is that of designing a tolerable armistice between the various contending factions within the community and of finding ways of raising effective force against those who break the armistice—whereas pacifism, as Niebuhr had decided, does in effect, for the sake of peace and order, finally advocate nothing other than surrender to maleficence. So at last he felt himself required to disclaim the whole pacifist program, and it is in his brilliant book of 1940, *Christianity and Power Politics,* that the grounds of his disavowal were most fully set forth.

Though his early writings were filled with theological digressions and *aperçus*, they did not in any systematic way define the basic theological perspectives wherewith Niebuhr was undertaking to build a line of relationship between ethics and politics. It was this task, however, which he began to undertake in his Rauschenbusch Lectures at the Colgate-Rochester Divinity School in the spring of 1934; and the resulting book that appeared in the following year, *An Interpretation of Christian Ethics,* may be thought of as the first major statement he produced in his capacity as Christian theologian. Here, the fundamental question with which he was wrestling concerned the kind of relevance that may be found in the ethic of *agape* to the proximate issues of moral and political discrimination that men confront in the historical order. The New Testament does, of course, present the utterly self-emptying love incarnate in Jesus of Nazareth as the final norm of human life. But such a norm, as Niebuhr argues, manifestly lacks any direct relevance to the concrete reality of man's social existence, for we are creatures of sin who are inveterately given to egoistical styles of self-definition—so that, in point of fact, the necessity we constantly face in the life of the human community is that of arranging, even in the most intimate relationships, balances of power that will permit mutually satisfactory forms of coexistence. The sacrificial heedlessness of the Cross does not, in other words, in any moment of human history represent an immediately realizable possibility for the moral life. Yet man, despite his habitually self-regarding and sinful propensities, is also endowed with a very radical kind of freedom. He "is the only mortal animal who knows that he is mortal, a fact which proves that in some sense he is not mortal. . . . [He] is the only creature imbedded in the flux of finitude who knows that this is his fate; which proves that in some sense this is not his fate."[7] He is one who must "relate all finite events to causes and consummations beyond

[7]Reinhold Niebuhr, *An Interpretation of Christian Ethics* (New York: Harper & Bros., 1935), p. 67.

themselves,"[8] and thus he is forever envisaging modes of order and harmony transcending the contingent realities of any immediate occasion. Which means that, though mortal and "imbedded in the flux of finitude," he stands always under ideal possibilities and can, therefore, find the ultimate ground of his life only in a transcendent norm. True, the profound improbity of the human heart makes it inevitable that we should be reduced to something like despair, when we confront this transcendent norm in the New Testament picture of Jesus as the Christ: yet, as Niebuhr suggests, it is just out of such despair that there may come what Saint Paul speaks of as "the godly sorrow [that] worketh repentance." So he concludes that, though the ethic of *agape* presents "an impossible ethical ideal," it is one which, nonetheless, may not simply be "relegated . . . to the world of transcendence," since always "it offers immediate possibilities of a higher good in every given situation."[9] In short, the law of love, though it holds forth a norm that surpasses our reach, prompts a scrutiny of our intentions and actions more searching than any appraisal they are likely to be subjected to at the level of a merely prudential morality.

It was along these lines that the argument of the Rauschenbusch Lectures proceeded, and the book of 1935 did indeed present a kind of provisional conspectus of the work that was to follow in the remaining years of the decade, in *Beyond Tragedy* (1937) and in *Christianity and Power Politics* (1940). For in these books he was steadily deepening the kind of analysis begun in the Rauschenbusch Lectures, of that state of contradiction in which man dwells—wherein, on the one hand, he finds the law of love to define the true essence of *humanitas* and, on the other hand, finds the human story to be one of consistent betrayal of that law. Which is to say that his writing at the end of the 'thirties gives evidence of his being ever more responsive in these years to "the great tradition" of the Fathers and the Reformers, and particularly of Augustine, for what his work of this period reveals, above all else, is an intention so to rehabilitate the classical doctrines of sin and forgiveness and reconciliation and grace as to make them the basic theorems of a realistic sociology and theory of politics. He was, of course, by popular journalism beginning to be swept under the umbrella (along with Karl Barth and Emil Brunner and Paul Tillich) of what was being called "Neo-Orthodoxy," and this clumsy counter no doubt obfuscates far more than it clarifies—though it may have the one salutary effect of reminding abecedarians that, for all their fidelity to theological tradition, none of these thinkers, and most especially Niebuhr himself, can be properly thought of as representing any sort of "fundamentalism." What is in fact one of the most notable aspects of Niebuhr's argument in *An Interpretation of Christian Ethics* and

[8]Ibid., p. 66.
[9]Ibid., p. 148.

in *Beyond Tragedy* is the stress he lays on the "mythical" character of Christian dogma. Yet, despite this insistently "neo-orthodox" element in his thought, he was very clearly moving to the right theologically, though all the while vigorously maintaining that the leftist character of his politics was an immediate corollary of his theological position, that trenchant critique of social injustice could only find its sure foundation in such a view as the Christian faith proposes of the radical contradiction between the law of love and the human actuality.

So profound an impact was he beginning to have on the theological scene that his colleagues in this country and abroad were by no means surprised when the University of Edinburgh invited him to hold the Gifford Lectureship in the spring and autumn of 1939, an appointment that had then been previously carried by only four other Americans —William James, Josiah Royce, William Ernest Hocking, and John Dewey. "When I [received the invitation]," as he said in an autobiographical essay of 1956, "I chose the only subject which I could have chosen, because the other fields of Christian thought were beyond my competence. I lectured on 'The Nature and Destiny of Man,' comparing Biblical with classical and modern conceptions of human nature and destiny."[10] And it is today the general consensus that, indeed, his Gifford Lectures on *The Nature and Destiny of Man* constitute his magnum opus and one of the masterpieces of modern theological literature.

The breadth of scope and the density of argument marking this central work of Niebuhr's career are such as to make it impossible to produce any swift résumé of all its diverse themes—of its many striking reinterpretations of important phases of philosophic and theological tradition, and of various crucial moments in intellectual and cultural history (Hellenism, Renaissance humanism, Romanticism, Marxism); of its brilliant reformulation of the Christological and eschatological motifs of Christian thought; and of numerous other strands of the total fabric. But the two volumes, when looked at in their entirety, would seem to have two main axes—namely, a theory of history, and what I have elsewhere spoken of as a "phenomenology of selfhood."[11] The former is given detailed and illuminating treatment by my collaborator, Professor Gilkey, and, since it provided the substructure of his political theory —for which Niebuhr is today most widely acclaimed—it is the specific phase of *The Nature and Destiny of Man* which is now apt to be most immediately in view. Yet that side of the Gifford Lectures which is likely to make the largest final claim on future arbiters of intellectual ferment in the first half of this century is that which entails the great feat of

---

[10]Reinhold Niebuhr, "Intellectual Autobiography," in *Reinhold Niebuhr*, ed. Kegley and Bretall, p. 9.

[11]Nathan A. Scott, Jr., *Reinhold Niebuhr*, Pamphlets on American Writers, no. 31 (Minneapolis: University of Minnesota Press, 1963), p. 31.

imagination represented by Niebuhr's analysis of the nature of selfhood. For it is in this dimension of his thought, as one of the great Christian "psychologists" of the modern period, that he most nearly perhaps proves his parity with Pascal and with Kierkegaard.

For Niebuhr, the critical datum with which any philosophical or theological anthropology must first reckon is the fact of man's being situated at a point of juncture between necessity and freedom, between nature and spirit. Human selfhood is grounded in a physical organism which is subject to all the vicissitudes and contingencies of the natural order: man is a radically finite creature who "needs air to breathe and space in which to abide,"[12] who must not be overly exposed to the summer's heat or the winter's cold: he is one whose perspectives are controlled by the relativities of social and cultural circumstance, and his life is but of short duration. Yet, frail though he be, he is not merely confined to his time and his place: his memory can span the ages, and his imagination can touch the fringes of eternity. Not only can he stand, as it were, above the structures and coherences of nature and history, making them the instruments of his intentionality: he can also take the measure of the creature who performs this act of transcendence, so that it becomes in turn an act of self-transcendence—which may proceed on into indeterminate degrees, as the self makes itself the object of its own thought.

Man is thus at once radically finite and radically free, and it is precisely in this condition of being suspended betwixt finitude and freedom that Niebuhr locates the essential "problematic" of selfhood. For man, like all other creatures, is

involved in the necessities and contingencies of nature; but unlike the animals he sees this situation and anticipates its perils. He seeks to protect himself against nature's contingencies; but he cannot do so without transgressing the limits which have been set for his life. Therefore all human life is involved in the sin of seeking security at the expense of other life. The perils of nature are thereby transmuted into the more grievous perils of human history. Or again: man's knowledge is limited by time and place. Yet it is not as limited as animal knowledge. The proof that it is not so limited is given by the fact that man knows something of these limits, which means that in some sense he transcends them. Man knows more than the immediate natural situation in which he stands, and he constantly seeks to understand his immediate situation in terms of a total situation. Yet he is unable to define the total human situation without colouring his definition with finite perspectives drawn from his immediate situation. The realization of the relativity of his knowledge subjects him to the peril of scepticism. The abyss of meaninglessness yawns on the brink of all his mighty spiritual endeavours. Therefore man is tempted to deny the limited character of his knowledge, and the finiteness of his perspectives. He pretends to have achieved a degree of knowledge which is beyond the limit of finite life. This is the

[12] Ibid.

"ideological taint" in which all human knowledge is involved and which is always something more than mere human ignorance. It is always partly an effort to hide that ignorance by pretension.[13]

In short, the psychological consequence of man's involvement in the paradox of finitude and freedom is that he is an anxious creature: he

is anxious not only because his life is limited and dependent and yet not so limited that he does not know of his limitations. He is also anxious because he does not know the limits of his possibilities. He can do nothing and regard it perfectly done, because higher possibilities are revealed in each achievement. All human actions stand under seemingly limitless possibilities. There are, of course, limits but it is difficult to gauge them from any immediate perspective. There is therefore no limit of achievement in any sphere of activity in which human history can rest with equanimity.[14]

The human condition, says Niebuhr, is like that of "the sailor, climbing the mast . . . with the abyss of the waves beneath him and the 'crow's nest' above him. He is anxious about both the end toward which he strives and the abyss of nothingness into which he may fall."[15] It is, indeed, something like a sense of "dizziness" that is induced by the ambiguity in which man is caught, by reason of his being subject at once to the conditions of finitude and freedom. And though Niebuhr does not conceive anxiety itself to posit the actuality of sin, he speaks of it as the *pre*condition and the "source of temptation," since it invites man either to seek some form of sensual self-indulgence as an escape from the anguish of freedom or to deny the contingent character of his existence by making the claim of absoluteness for what is in fact only finite and conditioned. "When anxiety has conceived, it brings forth both pride and sensuality. Man falls into pride, when he seeks to raise his contingent existence to unconditioned significance; he falls into sensuality, when he seeks to escape from his unlimited possibilities of freedom, from the perils and responsibilities of self-determination, by immersing himself into a 'mutable good,' by losing himself in some natural vitality."[16]

So it is, as the analysis of "the human condition" is elaborated by way of the great protocols of Christian theology, that the project advanced by the Gifford Lectures moves through its course with a pungency of vision and rhetoric that make a kind of prodigy in the literature of our time bearing on "the nature and destiny of man."

*   *   *

The years immediately following the publication of Niebuhr's Edin-

[13]Reinhold Niebuhr, *The Nature and Destiny of Man*, vol. 1 (New York: Charles Scribner's Sons, 1941), pp. 181–82.
[14]Ibid., p. 183.
[15]Ibid., p. 185.
[16]Ibid., p. 186.

burgh lectures (the first volume appearing in 1941, the second in 1943) were filled with large accomplishment and with large public recognitions. In addition to his teaching commitments at Union Seminary (where the eagerness of doctoral students to have him direct their dissertations resulted in his carrying heavy faculty responsibilities), he was preaching weekly in college and university chapels over the country, with a brilliance that agnostic dons found irresistible. As an associate editor of *The Nation,* he was regularly contributing political commentary to its pages (till at last his embarrassment at the naiveté of Freda Kirchwey's editorial policy regarding Stalinism led him to withdraw from her circle). He was himself editing two journals of social and political criticism, the fortnightly paper *Christianity and Crisis,* that he had established in 1941, and the quarterly *Christianity and Society,* which was the organ of the Fellowship of Socialist Christians; and both were periodicals widely read, not only by churchmen but also by large numbers of public men and intellectuals of liberal orientation. As a vice-president of the Liberal Party of New York State, he was deeply involved in negotiating the kind of "third force" it was attempting to introduce into the politics of New York City and the state at large. In 1941 he had become the first national chairman of the Union for Democratic Action, and, after it became the Americans for Democratic Action (ADA) in 1947, he remained one of its chief strategists. Through these years he was playing a key role in the establishment of such organizations as the Committee for Cultural Freedom, the American Association for a Democratic Germany, the American Christian Palestine Committee, and the Resettlement Campaign for Exiled Professionals. He was constantly moving back and forth across the Atlantic to lecture in universities abroad and to serve the World Council of Churches in various capacities. And, by the late 'forties, he had become one of the chief advisers to the State Department's Policy Planning Staff, on whose thought his impact was so deep that George Kennan, in looking back on that period (in which the Staff, established by General Marshall in 1947, was comprised of Paul H. Nitze, Louis J. Halle, C. B. Marshall, Dorothy Fosdick, and himself), has been led to say that Niebuhr was "the father of us all."[17] So it is no wonder that he was elected to that special academy—of the influential and the glamorous—superintended by *Time* magazine and that (to his discomfiture) his face became a frequent property of its covers and pages.

Yet, despite this immense range of activity in public life, the volume of his writing continued to be enormous. In, for example, the period between 1942 and 1952, apart from essays prepared for various books edited by others, he published 182 articles on theological and political

[17]Quoted in June Bingham, *Courage to Change: An Introduction to the Life and Thought of Reinhold Niebuhr* (New York: Charles Scribner's Sons, 1961), p. 368.

themes in such journals as *The Nation, Fortune,* the *Sewanee Review, Commentary, The Virginia Quarterly Review, Christianity and Crisis, The Reporter, The New Leader, Christianity and Society,* the *Spectator,* the *New Statesman and Nation, The Christian Century,* and the *Atlantic Monthly.* Two books devoted to an examination of the predicaments of democratic society—*The Children of Light and the Children of Darkness* (1944) and *The Irony of American History* (1952)—created a great stir, particularly amongst historians and political theorists. Though the book of 1952 is focused on the American tradition, both books were mainly calculated to rescue the democratic credo from "the excessively optimistic estimates of human nature . . . with which [it] . . . has been historically associated,"[18] in order that the perils besetting democratic culture in the troubled time that followed the close of the Second World War might be more soberly gauged. In 1946, he published *Discerning the Signs of the Times,* like *Beyond Tragedy* a collection of pieces adapting to essay form material originally designed for sermonic presentation in university chapels and undertaking to define the particular kind of poise which an eschatological faith may afford in a period when the realities of world politics offer little more than disappointed hopes and "calculated risks." And the year 1949 saw the publication of *Faith and History,* a great magisterial essay in the philosophy of history which retrieves and more rigorously expounds many of the central themes of his Gifford Lectures.

There had been occasional warnings over many years—in seizures of extreme fatigue—of the toll that his fierce schedules of work were taking; and at last, his great reserves of strength having been exhausted, in February 1952 he suffered the first in a series of small strokes that were for many months to threaten his life. Yet, finally, the attending physicians could only marvel at the stoutness of spirit with which this remarkably gallant man began slowly to recover. His convalescence was protracted, and some bit of paralysis remained in his left arm and hand. But he was eventually able to return to his classroom, and he did not withdraw from the Union Seminary faculty until the spring of 1960, when, in his sixty-eighth year, retirement was mandatory. He was never able to resume so hectic a program of work as he had followed prior to the onset of his illness, but, despite the great enervation it exacted, eleven books followed his collapse in 1952 at least three of which—*Christian Realism and Political Problems* (1953), *The Self and the Dramas of History* (1955), and *The Structure of Nations and Empires* (1959)—must be accounted amongst the major statements of his career.

Though the partial invalidism of his last years required him to live very quietly in the handsome old house in Stockbridge, Massachusetts, to

---

[18]Reinhold Niebuhr, *The Children of Light and the Children of Darkness: A Vindication of Democracy and a Critique of Its Traditional Defence* (New York: Charles Scribner's Sons, 1944), p. x.

which he had moved from his New York apartment, he preserved a passionate concern for all the important intellectual and political events of the turbulent 1960s. His gifted and beautiful wife Ursula, long a professor at Barnard College and chairman of its Department of Religion, had resigned her post, in order (as she would casually say, in the crisp English accent she had retained since coming to the States in the early 'thirties to be his student at Union Seminary, after taking a "first" in theology at Oxford) to devote herself to "Reinhold's health and happiness"; and her ministries kept him fully *engagé*. He offered the warmest partisanship to the civil rights struggle being carried forward by the Negro freedom movement and to the movements of resistance evoked by the country's misadventures in Southeast Asia. Nor was he forgotten. His (now) honorary chairmanship of ADA was by no means conceived to be a mere formality, and the stalwarts of this fellowship (still a significant force in the American 'sixties, though not so puissant as in an earlier period) regularly made their way to Stockbridge to seek counsel and encouragement, as did many of the most prestigious figures in the intellectual society of the nation. He was awarded the Presidential Medal of Freedom in 1964. And though he held honorary degrees from Glasgow and Oxford, from Harvard and Yale, and from scores of other universities, his profound affection for Jewry and the new state of Israel prompted him to be grateful for none so much as for the doctorate that President Avraham Harman of the Hebrew University traveled from Jerusalem to Stockbridge to bestow upon him in 1970.

Now, though, late in the eighth decade of his life, his strength was gone, and, at last, in his seventy-eighth year he died peacefully in his home at Stockbridge on Tuesday evening, June 1, 1971.

*   *   *

The frivolous experimentalism of American theology in the 1960s made it appear to be by no means unaffected, like so much else in cultural life, by the general Slump of the period. In one moment it was to be found sponsoring theologies "of the death of God," and in another moment theologies "of play," "of festivity," "of fantasy," and "of the psychedelic experience." It had joined the Dionysiac pack: its shamanistic tacticians were intending to be "swingers," and their impatience with anybody who questioned their "scenarios" for Paradise Now made them so heedless of the legacy of one like Reinhold Niebuhr that, for a time, he appeared to have been suddenly relegated to the discard. So it was also in the world of radical politics: there, too, a great passion for simplistic affirmation reigned, and, amidst the angers engendered by the Vietnam war and the strident new ethnicism, it began to be taken for granted—by the pundits, say, of *The New York Review* and the votaries of that brief enterprise called the New Left—that what the urgencies of the hour required above all else was a confidence in the rightness of one's own cause uncomplicated by any dubieties regarding its unilateralism or liability to distortion. And thus a representative figure like the young historian Christopher Lasch concluded that Niebuhr's "realism" could no longer speak with relevance to the contemporary scene, so trapped was it within its polemic against utopianism and its "preoccupation with the 'tragedy' and 'irony' of politics."[19] The Children of Light were wanting to maintain that the salvation of Lyndon Johnson's America was in the keeping of what Michael Harrington called "the conscience constituency,"[20] and Niebuhr's pragmatism—his insistence that a decent justice in the public realm can only be insured by a nicely adjusted system of countervailing powers as between the various constituencies—could finally, as certain arbiters claimed, have the effect merely of muting radical critique and of shoring up a repressive system.

As Professor Shinn's essay in this book is reminding us, however,

Niebuhr was never an unmitigated pragmatist. His was a pragmatism in a theological context, a pragmatism suffused with the doctrine of sin and tragedy, a pragmatism concerned to find proximate solutions to humanly insoluble problems. At the center of his theology was the cross of Christ, and he deeply resented any effort to interpret the cross pragmatically as a calculated device for achieving historical goals. But in the area of political ethics he repeatedly attacked dogmatic ideologies and asked for empirical and pragmatic assessment of actual possibilities.

It is, of course, difficult to measure the extent to which this whole mentality begins now to recede. But the enormous amount of research on his thought being currently done in the universities by doctoral students makes one indication of his power still to fascinate the young. In 1974 his legacy was discussed with an extraordinary intensity of interest in a major symposium of the American Political Science Association —which suggests perhaps that others also may now be inclined to accede to Hans Morgenthau's judgment, that, after Calhoun, he is "perhaps the only creative political philosopher [in American thought]. . . ."[21] And, in the world of contemporary theology, as the fads of the 'sixties begin already to be forgotten and the serious task is resumed of seeking a hermeneutic wherewith to demonstrate the continuing cogency of the perspectives on modern experience offered by the Christian faith, the pressure of Niebuhr's influence in his fields of theological work is everywhere a primary fact of the present scene.

[19]Christopher Lasch, *The New Radicalism in America* (New York: Alfred A. Knopf, Inc., 1965), p. 300.
[20]Michael Harrington, *Toward a Democratic Left: A Radical Program for a New Majority* (New York: Macmillan Co., 1968), p. 291.
[21]Hans J. Morgenthau, "The Influence of Reinhold Niebuhr in American Political Life and Thought," in *Reinhold Niebuhr: A Prophetic Voice in Our Time*, ed. Harold R. Landon (Greenwich, Conn.: Seabury Press, 1962), p. 109.

Introduction

So it seemed appropriate that the issue for the autumn of 1974 of *The Journal of Religion*[22] (whose editorship I share with Professors B. A. Gerrish and David Tracy) should be devoted to several reassessments of Niebuhr's thought, and it is these which comprise this book. Robert McAfee Brown presents a moving personal memoir that wonderfully conveys a sense of the greatness of the human being, of the modesty and generousness and charm that marked Niebuhr's personality. Kenneth W. Thompson delineates the extraordinary adroitness with which Niebuhr held in tension throughout his career his commitments to systematic intellectual work and to full participation in the forums of practical politics. Martin E. Marty, in his careful account of Niebuhr's interpretation of the various styles of American religion, explores an aspect of his concerns hitherto largely neglected. Langdon Gilkey, through his penetrating analysis of Niebuhr's interpretation of history, relates his thought to the new "theologies of liberation" being developed by such thinkers as Wolfhart Pannenberg, Jürgen Moltmann, and Johannes Metz. Franklin I. Gamwell clarifies the distinctively theological foundations of Niebuhr's ethical theory. And Roger L. Shinn presents a fresh estimate of his "political realism" in relation to recent styles of American radicalism.

It is hoped that this symposium may to some extent advance current reappropriation of one of the most impressive intellectual careers of this century. And the contributors are happy to dedicate the book to the great lady who was for forty years Reinhold Niebuhr's beloved wife and his devoted comrade in all undertakings.

[22]*The Journal of Religion* is issued by the Divinity School of the University of Chicago and published quarterly by the University of Chicago Press.

Reinhold Niebuhr: A Study in Humanity and Humility

Robert McAfee Brown

In the following pages many words are written about the greatness of Reinhold Niebuhr's mind, his wide-ranging intellect, his polemical brilliance, his acute political and pragmatic analyses, and the way that these and other gifts were always combined with the kind of "Christian realism" that he helped to fasten upon the American scene. But in the midst of these recollections of Niebuhr's brilliance and his place on the stage of American and world opinion, it is important to record another side of the man, a side that can be described by such words as "humanity" and "humility." I stress initially the notion of humility because during his public career Niebuhr was a man of such eminence, and of such flashing and polemical brilliance, that it would not have occurred to most people to describe him as humble. It needs to be stressed, therefore, that the man who so tellingly reacquainted a whole theological generation with the sin of pride was himself singularly free of that shortcoming.

This fact was brought home to me during my early days as a student at Union Theological seminary, during the height of World War II. The Niebuhrs had "open house" almost every Thursday evening, a high point of the student week that was always heavily attended, often by Niebuhr's most ardent disciples, a number of whom were not above correcting the master when they felt that he had not properly represented his own thought. On one such occasion there was a sharp and typically polemical discussion of pacifism in general and the pacifism of E. Stanley Jones in particular. It centered on the "naiveté" of Christian pacifists who assumed, in the midst of World War II, that pacifism would still "work." Niebuhr was sharing in the discussion with his accustomed vigor when all of a sudden he stopped, and in a very different tone of voice said, "But who am I to pass judgment on Stanley Jones? He's one of the great Christian saints of our time."

Reinhold Niebuhr: Humanity and Humility

As I reflect upon the dormitory discussions that used to take place at Union concerning pacifism in wartime, I wish that those of us who were taking Niebuhr very seriously had been able to display the same kind of humility and had learned to distinguish, in our own rather imitative polemics, between an attack on a position and an attack on a person.

How reassuring it was to us who studied under Niebuhr when he was at the height of his intellectual power and world eminence to discover that he had once been a pastor in a small church, that he too had run out of sermon ideas within a few weeks of accepting a charge and, most comforting of all, had hated making pastoral calls and like all of us had sometimes gone around the block three times before getting up nerve enough to ring the doorbell, still fervently hoping no one would be home. It was all there in *Leaves from the Notebook of a Tamed Cynic*—distressingly out of print in our seminary days, but eagerly devoured by all of us when a secondhand copy finally made its way into Hastings Hall.

The ability to wear his national and international honors lightly was never more apparent than during the months each summer that the Niebuhr family spent in the tiny town of Heath, Massachusetts, one of those amazing places in which, if you shake a given tree hard enough, at least six theologians will fall out. No matter what his summer schedule might be, Dr. Niebuhr would always preach at least once in the Heath Evangelical United Church. There could be no better indication of the ability of this sophisticated theologian to be a clear and direct parson, relating his preaching to the situation of the year-round congregation, than the sermons Niebuhr gave on such occasions. I remember one summer in particular when he had come back from some international gathering, and all of the "theological summer residents" in the town of Heath (who forsake their trees at eleven o'clock on Sunday morning) were ready for a typical Niebuhrian analysis of the state of the world. Niebuhr, however, chose to preach on the parable of the wheat and tares. After completing the reading of the gospel lesson, with its admonition not to pull up the weeds but to let them grow together with the good crop until the harvest, he began his sermon in terms that immediately identified with the New England farmers in the congregation: "This parable may be good theology, but it is certainly bad agriculture."

It might be noted for the record that a service at the Heath church was also the original occasion for what has since entered into the public domain with the rather unfortunate title of "the serenity prayer"—"O God, give us serenity to accept what cannot be changed, courage to change what should be changed, and wisdom to distinguish the one from the other." Niebuhr had jotted this down casually before a service he was conducting, and it has since, in a most extraordinary fashion, made its way into the religious folklore of our nation, subsequently being attributed to such diverse figures as Kurt Vonnegut and Adlai Stevenson, as well as being officially adopted by Alcoholics Anonymous.

Indeed, the dimension of Niebuhr that can be described by humility would have to stress Niebuhr the preacher and the pray-er. For in the pulpit, Niebuhr was not so much expounding his own insights about world politics as giving brilliant and highly original exegeses of biblical passages. These might, the first few times they made the university pulpit circuit, be a little long on sin and short on grace, for Niebuhr preached from brief notes, and the sermons, full of asides and scripture passages quoted from memory, would usually approach their time limit long before the analysis had been completed and the remedy proposed. But by the time they had been revised for publication and had made their way into such collections of "sermonic essays" as *Beyond Tragedy* (still perhaps the best introduction to Niebuhr) and *Discerning the Signs of the Times*, they were, if the allusion does not sound blasphemous, not only full of sin but "full of grace and truth" as well.

Sometimes spontaneity got the better of measured prose, and one of the most striking sermons Niebuhr ever gave in the Union Seminary Chapel dealt with the Pauline notion of becoming a "fool for Christ." In a typically Niebuhrian but perhaps unpulpit-like comment at the end of this sermon, he both challenged and convulsed his congregation by the statement, "There are many Christians who do not seem to know the difference between being a 'fool for Christ' and being a plain damn fool." Saint Paul with his sprinkling of "God forbids!" (probably better translated by Clarence Jordan in the *Cotton Patch Version of Paul's Epistles* as, "Hell no!") could hardly have disapproved.

In his more directly professional work as theologian and ethicist, Niebuhr is usually remembered for the crispness of his polemics and the vigor with which he could destroy a position contrary to his own. There is, indeed, a strong note of this in most of Niebuhr's writing, though in

3

later life he frequently deplored the sharpness of his earlier attacks and confessed in print his dismay at some youthful attacks on his later colleague at Union, Harry Emerson Fosdick. But it should be noticed by those who think of Niebuhr primarily in these terms that his main stance was not negative but positive; his negations were for the purpose of clearing the ground so that his affirmations could be more readily understood and accepted. I have always felt that it was unfortunate that the two volumes of his Gifford Lectures, *The Nature and Destiny of Man*, were published two years apart, for the first volume, "Human Nature" (1941), was indeed a brilliant polemical attack on most contemporary views of man, by means of which Niebuhr's firm place on the American theological scene was assured, but it did leave the impression that his main gifts lay in demolition. It was not until two years later that the second volume, "Human Destiny," appeared, in which he gave his own affirmative statement. But even that gap in time may in the long run help Niebuhr's communicability to later generations of students, for volume 1 was so strongly attacked for its stylistic obtuseness that Niebuhr delayed publication of volume 2 long enough to have Dr. Henry Sloane Coffin, president of Union Theological Seminary, unravel its sentences before they were committed to print, a labor of love Niebuhr acknowledged gratefully in the preface.

Even in the midst of his own polemics, however, there was a sense in which Niebuhr's own humility came through. This is evident in his comment about avoiding inordinate claims for one's position in relation to competing points of view. "We must," he said, "fight their falsehood with our truth, but we must also fight the falsehood in our truth." The ability both to admire and attack was never more evident than in Niebuhr's frequent oral and written jousts with his close friend and colleague, Paul Tillich. In his essay in the Kegley and Bretall volume, *The Theology of Paul Tillich*, Niebuhr concludes with the image of those who walk on the tightrope between metaphysics and theology. He points out that Tillich was a virtuoso in walking this tightrope, though he was one who occasionally, so Niebuhr felt, suffered a fall. But he then concludes, in typically characteristic Niebuhrian fashion, "The fall may be noticed by some humble pedestrians who lack every gift to perform the task themselves."

A similar kind of recognition is present in a comment he once made in class about how Virginia Woolf used to be terribly nervous and threatened and upset when reviews of her latest book would begin to appear. Material, obviously, for vintage comments by Niebuhr about human fear, dread, *angst,* and all the other Kierkegaardian traits he could catalog so well, against which he then put the Pauline comment, "For me it is a small thing to be judged of man . . . he that judgeth me is the Lord." And then, in what was a clear departure from the outline, Niebuhr said, "How foolish it was for Virginia Woolf to be so upset by reviews. But as soon as I say that, I realize I am exactly the same way myself."

A typical example of Niebuhr's humanity is contained in a hitherto unrecorded episode that occurred at the end of a summer when he had returned from a long European trip. Niebuhr arrived back in the United States to a mountain of mail, and in going through it came across a letter from a former student who had just been released from the navy chaplaincy and was serving in a parish in a town in Massachusetts. The student, after describing the difference between a ministry in the navy and a ministry in a small New England town, commented on how much he and his wife were enjoying biking around the town and countryside to pay pastoral calls. Niebuhr promptly dispatched a letter to the young minister pointing out that he was about to return to New York for the fall and winter and would have no need for his rather ancient Ford until the following summer. Would it be of use during the New England winter, when bicycle riding would be less feasible? . . . The fact that in the midst of a frantically busy life, and a desk groaning with unanswered mail, it would occur to Niebuhr to make such a gesture was only typical of the man. There are countless other students who could recall similar episodes; the reason I have the facts on this one is that I was the student to whom the welcome letter came. (One of my ministerial friends, who was not enamored of Niebuhr's theology, spoke of me during my tenure in the driver's seat of Niebuhr's Ford as "sitting in the seat of the scornful," but I was more inclined to view the experience as my closest approach to apostolic succession.)

It was characteristic of Niebuhr that he could learn from all sorts and conditions of men and that he did not try to suggest that all of his theological insights had come from Augustine or Kierkegaard or Jeremiah or Paul. He recounts in an autobiographical essay that as a young pastor his real understanding of the meaning of the Christian faith came through the experience in his Detroit parish of seeing two elderly women approach death—one doing so in a grasping and resentful fashion, making harsh demands upon her friends, while the other approached death with a grace and serenity that were immensely impressive to the young pastor. The lesson stayed with Niebuhr, for, at the time of his own serious stroke in 1952, he recalls that during the days when he was hovering between life and death the words that he most frequently remembered, and that sustained him through that period, were those of Saint Paul: "If we live, we live to the Lord and if we die, we die to the Lord; so then, whether we live or whether we die, we are the Lord's" (Rom. 14:8).

There were surely many times during the subsequent eighteen years when this kind of grace must have been hard to maintain, and it would be the most unrealistic (and un-Niebuhrian) kind of sentimentality to pretend that he was not often depressed by the severe limitations that his partial paralysis placed upon him. This frequently made things difficult for his family and friends, but those who knew Niebuhr before the stroke and in the period after the stroke could never fail to be impressed by the way in which this man, once so extraordinarily vigorous and active, was able to cope with an extremely limited kind of physical existence in which the margins of physical reserve were limited to short periods of time, so that strength had to be husbanded for those moments when a speech was to be given or an essay written, or even, during the last few years, when a brief conversation was to take place. There was indeed a peace and serenity that flowed from the life of this once vigorous and now frail human being who could look back over his early years and regret some impetuous statements, but who, when the follies of certain of our national leaders were brought into the conversation, could also recapture his former prophetic denunciation of the pride and pretention of the powerful leaders of powerful nations. (Even at the end, the words "Richard Nixon" could evoke from Niebuhr refreshing and hearty epithets.)

Niebuhr will probably be remembered most as a prophet and social critic. But full justice will not be done until he is also remembered as priest and pastor—one who not only made pragmatic political judgments but also meditated on the mystery of human existence and passed on to those who knew him a deep wisdom born not of sophistication but of humility. Indeed, his greatest gift was probably his ability to combine these roles, so that biblical insights could be related to the common market, and highly technical political analysis could be informed in midstream by such insights as the following:

"Nothing that is worth doing can be achieved in our lifetime; therefore we must be saved by hope. Nothing which is true or beautiful or good makes complete sense in any immediate context of history; therefore we must be saved by faith. Nothing we do, however virtuous, can be accomplished alone; therefore we must be saved by love. No virtuous act is quite as virtuous from the standpoint of our friend or foe as it is from our standpoint; therefore we must be saved by the final form of love which is forgiveness." [1]

During World War II, one of Niebuhr's former students was reported missing in action, and Niebuhr preached a sermon in the seminary chapel about the meaning of this event. He concluded by saying of the student, "His fragrance was as the fragrance of the flowers, who do not know that they are fragrant." There could be no more fitting epitaph for Niebuhr himself.

NOTE.—In a few places Niebuhr indulged in autobiographical reflections, and these are well worth renewed attention on the part of those who return to a study of his substantive thought. *Leaves from the Notebook of a Tamed Cynic* (New York: Meridian Books, 1929) carries the reader through the Detroit parish to the departure for Union Theological Seminary. He offers an "Intellectual Autobiography" at the beginning of Kegley and Bretall, *Reinhold Niebuhr: His Religious, Social, and Political Thought* ([New York: Macmillan Co., 1956], pp. 3–23), and has an "autobiographical introduction" entitled "Changing Perspectives" in *Man's Nature and His Communities* ([New York: Charles Scribner's Sons, 1965], pp. 15–29), reflecting on shifts in his thinking and method. His interview with Patrick Granfield in Granfield's *Theologians at Work* ([New York: Macmillan Co., 1967], pp. 51–68) is full of autobiographical reminiscences. Of all the writings about Niebuhr, the fullest biographical material is found in June Bingham, *The Courage to Change* (New York: Charles Scribner's Sons, 1961).

---

[1] Reinhold Niebuhr, *The Irony of American History* (New York: Charles Scribner's Sons, 1952), p. 63.

Reinhold Niebuhr: Public Theology and the American Experience

Martin E. Marty

> The character of both nations and individuals may be defined as a pattern of consistent behavior, created on the one hand by an original ethnic, geographic and cultural endowment, and on the other hand by the vicissitudes of history, which shape and reshape, purify, corrupt and transmute this endowment.
>
> We are always part of the drama of life which we behold; and the emotions of the drama therefore color our beholding.
>
> [REINHOLD NIEBUHR][1]

ECCLESIASTICAL AND NATIONAL TRADITIONS

The main strand of American religious thought has drawn together the work of various figures who have interpreted the nation's religious experience, practice, and behavior in the light of some sort of transcendent reference. Roman Catholic theology in its most formal sense was not really free to do this until the middle of the twentieth century. But earlier Catholicism also included various popular figures and publicists—one thinks of Father Isaac Hecker or Orestes Brownson—who in informal ways made their contribution. Jewish thought has been consistently circumstantial, incorporating frequent references to the meaning of Judaism in America. In the course of the 1960s many theologians in the black community informed their contemporaries about the long lineage of reflection on the value of their peoples' experience in the new world.

The strand has been most consistently visible at the point of juncture between certain styles of Protestant thought and the representation of a

[1] First quotation from Reinhold Niebuhr and Alan Heimert, *A Nation So Conceived: Reflections on the History of America* (New York: Charles Scribner's Sons, 1963), p. 7 (hereinafter cited as *NSC*); second from Reinhold Niebuhr, *Discerning the Signs of the Times: Sermons for Today and Tomorrow* (New York: Charles Scribner's Sons, 1946), p. 10 (hereinafter cited as *DST*). Unless otherwise noted, all books cited are by Reinhold Niebuhr.

"religion of the Republic" which drew on Enlightenment resources. While the nation has produced a number of philosophers of religion who have written without much reference to situation, the more characteristic thinkers have taken on themselves the burden of interpreting experience and behavior as these have been embodied in religious groups and in the nation itself.

From the ecclesiastical side the great colonial focus was Jonathan Edwards, whose philosophy was shaped in constant reference to his painstaking observation of people in the midst of their conversion and awakening. Book titles such as *A Faithful Narrative of the Surprising Work of God etc.* or *Religious Affections* are typical of his empirical concerns. His charter for a fresh mode of theology was to have been "a great work, which I call a *History of the Work of Redemption*, a body of divinity in an entirely new method, being thrown into the form of a history."[2] In sermonic outline it concluded with reference to the awakenings in America and in Edwards's own ministry.

More than a century later Horace Bushnell, working out of a pastorate at Hartford, Connecticut, not many miles downriver from Edwards's Northampton, Massachusetts, used the raw material of his own contemporaries' religious behavior and experience to fashion his seminal *Christian Nurture* (1861) and other works which were theological reflections on alternatives to revivalism. Similarly, half a century later, Walter Rauschenbusch represented another significant turn in what came to be called the Social Gospel. His situation began with a ministry in Hell's Kitchen in New York and became one of observation of and participation in various seminary-based attempts to alter social circumstances. His *Christianity and the Social Crisis* (1907) and *Christianizing the Social Order* (1912) were in part theological extrapolations on these perceptions.

If Edwards, Bushnell, and Rauschenbusch represent what might be called public theology from the churches' side, their contemporaries Benjamin Franklin (or, later, Thomas Jefferson), Abraham Lincoln, and Woodrow Wilson used specifically deistic or theological materials in order to make sense of the American experience.[3] They were in

---

[2] Edwards is quoted by Sidney H. Rooy (*The Theology of Missions in the Puritan Tradition* [Grand Rapids, Mich.: William B. Eerdmans Publishing Co., 1965], p. 294) in an extensive passage on *A History of the Work of Redemption*.

[3] See, e.g., the somewhat dated James M. Stifler, *The Religion of Benjamin Franklin* (New York, 1925); Adrienne Koch, *Power, Morals, and the Founding Fathers* (Ithaca, N.Y.: Cornell University Press, 1961); G. Adolf Koch, *Religion of the American Enlightenment* (New York: Thomas Y. Crowell Co., 1968 [first published in 1933]);

every case uncommonly informed about the practices of religious people in the churches. They also looked for what appeared to them to be a broader and eventually deeper repository of religious motifs: the nation itself. Just as there have been more abstract and acontextual philosophers of religion than those cited here, so, too, there have been political philosophers who reasoned without much reference to their American circumstances. Their impact has been highly secondary to that of these statesmen-philosophers who served as public theologians.

THE TWENTIETH CENTURY: REINHOLD NIEBUHR AS MODEL

In the middle third of the twentieth century these two traditions came together in one person as never before through the career of Reinhold Niebuhr. His first book appeared in 1927, but at the turn to the second third of the century, with *Moral Man and Immoral Society* in 1932, his impact first began to be widely felt. A third of a century later in 1965—though editors were still to bring forth a couple of compilations from his earlier work—his literary career began to come to terminus in *Man's Nature and His Communities*. Its introduction detailed his debt to the practitioners of religion in the American environment. After several years of relative confinement because of ill health, he died in 1971. He and his brother, H. Richard Niebuhr (whose *The Social Sources of Denominationalism* and *The Kingdom of God in America* [1935] have been as determinative as many of Reinhold's essays on national themes),[4] towered over all other native-born theologians in their time. Together they offer the best personal paradigms of the emerging American public theology style.

Given Reinhold Niebuhr's book titles and main subjects, it may seem to be gratuitous to name him the century's foremost interpreter of American religious social behavior. Yet this has been a neglected

---

Paul F. Boller, Jr., *George Washington and Religion* (Dallas: Southern Methodist University Press, 1963); Robert M. Healey, *Jefferson on Religion in Public Education* (New Haven, Conn.: Yale University Press, 1962); Elton Trueblood, *Abraham Lincoln: Theologian of American Anguish* (New York: Harper & Row, 1972); William J. Wolf, *The Almost Chosen People: A Study of the Religion of Abraham Lincoln* (Garden City, N.Y.: Doubleday & Co., 1959); Robert S. Alley, *So Help Me God: Religion and the Presidency, Wilson to Nixon* (Richmond, Va.: John Knox Press, 1972); John M. Mulder, "Wilson the Preacher: The 1905 Baccalaureate Sermon," *Journal of Presbyterian History* 51, no. 3 (Fall 1973): 267 ff.

[4] H. Richard Niebuhr, *The Social Sources of Denominationalism* (New York: Henry Holt & Co., 1929) is a particularly valuable study of class-based religious collective behavior.

theme, one to which the numerous major interpretations of Niebuhr make scant and sometimes even apologetic reference. The reasons for this slighting are manifold. First, Niebuhr himself was surprisingly diffident and reticent, despite the range of his public commitments, to make the kind of autobiographical comment out of which interpretations based on his situation would grow. Almost every analyst is moved to comment on Niebuhr's reluctance to place himself visibly near the center of his work.

He could not completely and permanently avoid such references. His first book was dedicated to his pastor father and to his mother "who for twelve years has shared with me the work of a Christian pastorate," one which was memorialized in his most nearly autobiographical work, a sketchbook called *Leaves from the Notebooks of a Tamed Cynic*. He dedicated that book to his "friends and former co-workers in Bethel Evangelical Church, Detroit, Michigan," [5] where he had spent thirteen years of formative ministerial life. After his move in 1928 to New York's Union Theological Seminary, the locus of his subsequent career, the number of specific parochial comments progressively declined.

Only occasional later references reminded Niebuhr's readers of this factor in his life. In a rare twenty-page "Intellectual Autobiography" he acknowledged that the Detroit "facts determined my development more than any books which I may have read." [6] When autobiography was almost forced out of him in a *Christian Century* series in 1939 he alerted his readers: "Such theological convictions which I hold today began to dawn upon me during the end of a pastorate in a great industrial city." There he had seen how irrelevant simple moral homilies were in the realm of "human actions or attitudes in any problem of collective behavior." Even at Union "the gradual unfolding of my theological ideas [had] come not so much through study as through the pressure of world events." [7]

After his interpreters pay lip service to his own self-interpretative clues, they usually move on to formal analysis of his theological and

[5] The first quote is from *Does Civilization Need Religion?* (New York: Macmillan Co., 1927), dedication page (hereinafter cited as *DCNR*); the second from *Leaves from the Notebook of a Tamed Cynic* (New York: Living Age, 1957 [first published in 1929]), dedication page (hereinafter cited as *LNTC*).

[6] "Intellectual Autobiography," in *Reinhold Niebuhr: His Religious, Social, and Political Thought*, ed. Charles W. Kegley and Robert W. Bretall (New York: Macmillan Co., 1962), p. 5.

[7] "Ten Years That Shook My World," *Christian Century*, April 26, 1939, p. 545.

philosophical ideas on an almost entirely literary base of reference. Some of this skewing may be the result of their own predilections for discerning as more enduring the styles characteristically associated with historic European theology. Or they may be dismissing his circumstantial thought as being the ephemeral context out of which the permanent more abstract philosophical work emerged.

Niebuhr himself often threw people off the trail not only because of the paucity of autobiographical references, but because some of his major works took on an apparently more abstract character. His most solid and most studied book is *The Nature and Destiny of Man*,[8] the Gifford Lectures delivered in Scotland where an American accounting would have been largely beside the point. Yet hundreds of editorials and journalistic occasional pieces rich in American comment went into the background of that formal work. The American references in his other works preoccupy us here.

PHILOSOPHER OF AMERICAN PRAXIS

For all the range of his topics, Reinhold Niebuhr's thought was grounded in his perception that he was a servant of and, in a sense, a prophet to America-in-*praxis*. He conceived America as a nation of behavers and experiencers and not very often as theorists about their belief. But his reportorial perceptions were never reproduced as ends in themselves. Instead, he turned them into much of the stuff of his theology.

This "Professor of Applied Christianity" dealt constantly with the language of a believing and practicing ecclesiastical and national community. His primal vision as "a kind of circuit rider" in a secular age was that of one who had "never been very competent in the nice points of pure theology." He confessed that he had "not been sufficiently interested . . . to acquire the competence." He shared Tocqueville's observation of "the strong pragmatic interest of American Christianity in comparison with European Christianity," a distinction he thought to be valid a century later. When the "stricter sects of theologians in Europe" goaded Niebuhr to prove that his "interests were theological rather than practical or 'apologetic'" he made no defense, "partly

[8] *The Nature and Destiny of Man: A Christian Interpretation* (New York: Charles Scribner's Sons, 1948 [vol. 1 first published in 1942, vol. 2 in 1943]) (hereinafter cited as *NDM*.) Significantly, this is the single major work by Niebuhr that is not cited in the present essay; the only other noncited Niebuhr book is the more ephemeral *The Contribution of Religion to Social Work* (New York: Columbia University Press, 1932).

because I thought the point was well taken and partly because the distinction did not interest me." [9] So much for page 1 of his intellectual autobiography. A billboard could hardly have made the point more boldly.

Niebuhr's historic allusions displayed his consistency. When he contrasted his generation with Rauschenbusch's, he noted that the "difference was created not by the triumph of one philosophy over another or by the triumph of Comte over Spencer, but by the beneficent play of cultural and social forces in a free society. In this development, creeds and dogmas were transmuted into a wisdom better than that possessed by any dogmas." [10] His recall of the industrializing generation in America was not of theorists but of "American go-getters." [11]

Niebuhr could mourn the failure of good ideas in America. He was constantly critical of the way Puritans in practice corrupted their idea of taking "prosperity and adversity in its stride [into] a religion which became preoccupied with the prosperity of the new community." In doing so they came to see Jefferson's "'useful knowledge' as the only valuable knowledge," it was "knowledge 'applied to common purposes of life.'" [12]

The Irony of American History developed this theme most extensively. Chapter 5, titled "The Triumph of Experience over Dogma," condensed the Niebuhrian approach. Thus in the presumably ideological clash with Marxist nations, the fact that Americans developed reasonable degrees of justice was "due primarily to our highly favored circumstances"—the wealth of natural resources, and the like. The author then moved on to legitimate discussion of some ideological dimensions, but even there he remarked on how American practice compromised ideology, dogma, and theory. When housing, medicine, and social security became matters of public and political policy, "all this [was] accomplished on a purely pragmatic basis, without the ideological baggage which European labor carried." [13]

[9] See Kegley and Bretall, p. 3.

[10] *Faith and Politics: A Commentary of Religious, Social and Political Thought in a Technological Age,* ed. Ronald H. Stone (New York: George Braziller, Inc., 1968), p. 41 (hereinafter cited as *FP*).

[11] *The Children of Light and the Children of Darkness* (New York: Charles Scribner's Sons, 1945), p. 33 (hereinafter cited as *CLCD*).

[12] *The Irony of American History* (New York: Charles Scribner's Sons, 1952), p. 49 (hereinafter cited as *IAH*).

[13] Ibid., pp. 84–85, 91, 100.

As in national affairs, so in religion the affective and observable side mattered most to his compatriots. Niebuhr liked to quote the *London Times Literary Supplement* on the doctrinal point he had done more than any contemporary to revive: "The doctrine of original sin is the only empirically verifiable doctrine of Christian faith." One Niebuhrian interpreter took a line from James Thurber to talk about that chief visible doctrine in the peoples' behavioral pattern: "We all have our flaws, . . . and mine is being wicked." The Union Seminary theologian became the chief chronicler of American structural wickedness and of the relative justice that was achieved in spite of it.[14]

The abstract sphere represented cowardice and escape. In the earliest stages of his career Niebuhr had observed his own behavior to note how hard it was to amass courage so that one could deal with the concrete in religious communities: "One of the most fruitful sources of self-deception in the ministry is the proclamation of great ideals and principles without any clue to their relation to the controversial issues of the day. . . . I have myself too frequently avoided the specific application of general principles to controversial situations to be able to deny what really goes on in the mind of the preacher when he is doing this."[15] His later career made him ever less vulnerable to such a point of self-accusation.

THE RELOCATION OF THEOLOGY

Where did this love of the concrete and historical pattern leave religious thought? For Niebuhr, theology was simply relocated. He possessed a rare gift for relating idea to circumstance. The circumstances might change, but the ideas born of reflection on them could survive and be transformed. Thus when in 1960 he reintroduced his book from 1932 for fresh publication, he had to say that "naturally many of its references are dated," but "despite these dated references I consented to the republication of the book because I still believe that the central thesis of the book is important and I am still committed to it." Though he had changed his mind about many things in almost

---

[14] *Man's Nature and His Communities: Essays on the Dynamics and Enigmas of Man's Personal and Social Existence* (New York: Charles Scribner's Sons, 1965), p. 14 (hereinafter cited as *MNHC*). The Thurber citation is from Holtan P. Odegard, *Sin and Science: Reinhold Niebuhr as Political Theologian* (Yellow Springs, Ohio: Antioch Press, 1956), p. 11.

[15] *LNTC*, pp. 218–19.

three decades, he thought that "our contemporary experience validates rather than refutes the basic thesis."[16]

While he admitted that he had experienced "boredom with epistemology" as a Yale student, he later found it necessary to interpret his practical experience in theological terms.[17] Niebuhr knew how little the churches regarded such terms. "Here [in Detroit] I have been all these years in a conservative communion and have never had a squabble about theology."[18] Liberalism in the social realm was what always got his colleagues in trouble. Yet he himself had a positive appreciation of dogma and its history. It has "achieved a hated connotation in the lexicon of modernity, for it connotes the arbitrary assertion of what can not be proved scientifically. As a matter of fact, it was intended to avoid the arbitrariness of private interpretation and *to assure the 'public' character of the truth*. . . . Dogma, at its best, represents the consensus of a covenant community which lives upon the basis of common convictions and commitments" (emphasis mine).[19]

Niebuhr's own movement had been from practice through ethics toward theology. His awakening first came at Detroit through his temporary abandonment of the idea of "worrying so much about the intellectual problems of religion" when he began "to explore some of its ethical problems."[20] His first book depicted this movement through his judgment that "morality is as much the root as the fruit of religion; for religious sentiment develops out of moral experience, and religious convictions are the logic by which moral life justifies itself. . . . If religion is senescent in modern civilization, its social importance is as responsible for its decline as is its metaphysical maladjustment." Metaphysical thought could be a luxury, since it was a characteristic of "those classes which are not sensitive enough to feel and not unfortunate enough to suffer from the moral limitations of modern society. . . . The fact is that more men in our modern era are irreligious because religion has failed to make civilization ethical than because it has failed to maintain its intellectual respectability. For every person who disavows religion because some ancient and unrevised dogma outrages his intelligence, several become irreligious because

[16] *Moral Man and Immoral Society* (New York: Charles Scribner's Sons, 1960 [first published in 1932]), p. ix (hereinafter cited as *MMIS*).

[17] Kegley and Bretall, p. 4.

[18] *LNTC*, p. 59.

[19] *The Self and the Dramas of History* (New York: Charles Scribner's Sons, 1955), pp. 92–93 (hereinafter cited as *SDH*).

[20] *LNTC*, p. 45.

the social importance of religion outrages their conscience." Yet "the metaphysical problem of religion cannot be depreciated," for religion must be able to impress the minds of moderns with the essential plausibility of its fundamental affirmations.[21]

Throughout his later career, then, Niebuhr appropriated behavioral and ethical perceptions while his thought took on an increasingly metaphysical guise. In his later formal works the constant references are to Aquinas and Aristotle and Augustine or to Calvin and Hegel and Marx more than to the industrialists of Detroit or the seminarians of Morningside Heights. The *use* he made of these major thinkers is what was most significant. He readily admitted that he rarely studied them painstakingly for their own sakes. Rather he plundered their thought for that in them which could be reflected back into the American moral community.

THE DOCTRINE OR PRACTICE OF THE CHURCH

Niebuhr's thought was shaped by his vision of the American religious circumstance. Grasping the substance of that vision is important for any assessment of his role or for further development of the charter and vocation of any public theologian. Since Niebuhr was not a reporter but a transformer, it is not surprising to note that he dealt with virtual stereotypes of his contemporaries' behavioral patterns in their religious communities. He was quite uninterested in idiosyncratic or exceptional experience. He came to treat religious social behavior on nomothetic lines. He lacked the historians' taste for surprise and serendipity. People were expected to act in certain ways depending upon their situations and classes. They had to be able to be counted on almost as if they existed for the interpretations Niebuhr would provide. What he lacked in historical finesse he gained in social power.

He never developed an extensive ecclesiology. To quote John Bennett: "Niebuhr is basically a theologian who sees the implications of his theology for Christian ethics, but he has never addressed himself primarily to the Church as Church." "I doubt if we can make a very clear distinction between the substance of what he says explicitly as a theologian and churchman, and what he says when he speaks to the public." "Most of the critics of Niebuhr, whenever they write criticism, generally say he doesn't have a doctrine of the Church."[22]

[21] *DCNR*, pp. 12–16.
[22] Harold R. Landon, ed., *Reinhold Niebuhr: A Prophetic Voice in Our Time* (New York: Seaburg Press, 1962), pp. 61–62, 82.

Wilhelm Pauck "wondered about Niebuhr's ecclesiology, church-manship, *not in the practical sense . . . but more in the theological sense*" (emphasis mine). Pauck thought that Niebuhr had a "strangely spiritual concept of the Church."[23] (Niebuhr had strangely spiritual concepts of hardly anything. He merely had an undeveloped sense of or curiosity about the borders of the church.) Harold R. Landon defended Niebuhr for having held in practice a concept similar to that of Paul Tillich's "latent church" and for having served the church faithfully without having developed a corresponding doctrine. But Landon could also cite a succinct and significant statement on the church from *Beyond Tragedy*. Niebuhr there had said that "the Church is that place in human society where men are disturbed by the word of the eternal God . . . it is also the place where the word of mercy, reconciliation and consolation is heard. . . . The Church is the place in human society where the kingdom of God impinges upon all human enterprises through the divine word, and where the grace of God is made available to those who have accepted his judgment."[24]

Another editor added to the defense by eventually culling a great number of Niebuhrian essays that had reference to the church and publishing them as *Essays in Applied Christianity*. In that collection D. B. Robertson succeeded in showing how frequent were Niebuhr's ecclesiastical preoccupations but failed to show him much devoted to definition of the subject.[25]

If Niebuhr produced and employed stereotypes, this was not because he felt that once one reduced behavior to patterned outline, it could be used for simple prediction: "No scientific investigations of past behavior can become the basis of predictions of future behavior." He cautioned against trying to reduce the drama of history's confusion to some kind of simple meaning. Biography serves to disrupt "the analysis of uniformities and recurrences of behavior under like conditions." He considered the biographical and personal factor a good counter to determinism in social sciences: "The impulse to falsify the

23 Ibid., pp. 80–81.

24 Ibid., pp. 19–20; *Beyond Tragedy: Essays on the Christian Interpretation of History* (New York: Charles Scribner's Sons, 1965 [first published 1937]), p. 62 (hereinafter cited as *BT*).

25 *Essays in Applied Christianity*, ed. D. B. Robertson (New York: Living Age Books, 1958) (hereinafter cited as *EAC*), includes the following essays: in part 1, "The Weakness of Common Worship in American Protestantism"; in part 2, "Can the Church Give a 'Moral Lead'?" in part 5, "The Church and the Churches: The Ecumenical Movement."

facts in order to bring them into a comprehensible pattern assails the scientists who try to manage detailed facts and small patterns. Another analogous temptation assails the philosophers and ontologists who try to make sense out of the larger patterns of history and to comprehend the whole drama of history as meaningful."[26] In many respects Niebuhr can himself be accused of falling into both temptations because of his broad level of generalization and his reluctance to deal with exceptions to patterns. The picture of religious community that came to him in the beginning of his career stayed with him to the end, however mellowed he was by the time of his last book.

Though there are notable exceptions, that vision was often informed more by Marxian than Weberian analytic tools. That is, Niebuhr less readily saw the consequences of religious belief in, say, the Puritan community. More frequently he isolated the status, class, and context of a community and then elaborated on the almost inevitable character its religious ideology would take. This debt to Marx he acknowledged, however scornful of imposed Marxist ideology he was to become. "In a sense the word of Marx is true: 'The beginning of all criticism is the criticism of religion. For it is on this ultimate level that the pretensions of men reach their most absurd form. The final sin is always committed in the name of religion.'" Thereupon he diagnosed these sins on Marxian lines, seeing religion as the sanction of capitalist order or noting that many in the church declared politics to be irrelevant to the religious life or seeing part of the church to be content with "insufferable sentimentality," or, finally, with being legalistic.[27]

He could then turn around and comment on the Marxian short-sightedness for having seen religion as a "pie in the sky" refuge from the world, whereas in America it was actually used to enhance and legitimate worldliness and material prosperity.[28]

THE OBSERVATION OF COLLECTIVE BEHAVIOR

To see Reinhold Niebuhr, Professor of Applied Christianity, as a theologian who wrote theology out of his observation of America's collective religious behavior might lead one to treat him as a "theologian with the theology left out." His empirical sense; his choice of theological themes based upon what he considered to be a relevant address to the

[26] *SDH*, pp. 47, 49.

[27] *Christian Realism and Political Problems* (New York: Charles Scribner's Sons, 1953), pp. 109–10 (hereinafter cited as *CRPP*).

[28] *IAH*, pp. 54–55.

human situation; his journalistic avocation; his involvement with contemporary policymakers—all these prevent one from seeing him as an ivory-tower dweller with abstractions. When he dealt with churchly or national religious behavior, he did so without explicit reference to a literary tradition. Almost everything was based on observation. Proper nouns in these paragraphs and chapters were rare. He cited no major figures and seemed to be influenced by few. Niebuhr used his own eyes and assumed that readers saw the religious world roughly as he did. All he need do was convince them that what he did with the observation was appropriate.

His rather gloomy *Reflections on the End of an Era* (1934) included passages which showed that he was not content with what he saw. He looked for more reason and less impulse in religion, but knew that not much reason made its way into collective behavior. The social mechanisms of a commercial civilization "prevent the modern man from realizing that collective behavior is primarily impulsive, that its impulses are heedless and undirected and that will-to-live of every individual and social organism is easily transmuted into an imperial will-to-power." In that realm, "the dominance of reason over impulse is much more tentative and insecure than modern culture realizes." Hence, the dangers of pretension and pride in the collective life of the religious organization or the nation. The Pauline confession, "The good which I would I do not: but the evil which I would not, that I do," is *"perennially justified by human experience, particularly in collective human behavior"* (emphasis mine).[29]

Niebuhr himself did resist a simple determinism based on impulses and that will-to-power rooted in collective behavioral patterns. In his later years that resistance was reflected in a polemic against the behavioralism of B. F. Skinner, the psychologist author of *Walden Two*. At other times he reacted against a simple cultural relativism based on the observation of attitudes or customs, along with reductionist psychosocial explanations derived from Freudian and quasi-Freudian thought. He ranked Freudianism with Marxism in this respect, overlooking perhaps the degree to which Marxian economic determinisms tended to color his own often stereotypical views of behavior in American religion.[30]

That Niebuhr lacked a "doctrine of the Church" in a developed

[29] *Reflections on the End of an Era* (New York: Charles Scribner's Sons, 1934), pp. 4–5, 30.
[30] *SDH*, pp. 132, 143.

sense is obvious; that he outlined a complete sociology of the church is just as patent.[31] It is possible to trace almost every eventually developed view of the religious community in action back to his root experience in the Detroit parish. There he learned the limits of prophecy in the politics of the parish: "You can't rush into a congregation which has been fed from its very infancy on the individualistic ethic of Protestantism and which is immersed in a civilization where ethical individualism runs riot, and expect to develop a social conscience among the people in two weeks. Nor have you a right to insinuate that they are all hypocrites just because they don't see what you see."

In the parish he came to the conclusion that prophets almost have to be itinerants: "Critics of the church think we preachers are afraid to tell the truth because we are economically dependent upon the people of the church. There is something in that, but it does not quite get to the root of the matter. . . . I think the real clue to the tameness of a preacher is the difficulty one finds in telling unpleasant truths to people whom one has learned to love." In the introduction to the book that finds him reflecting on parish experience, there is a patient and tender note that disappeared when he became an itinerant prophet at Union Theological Seminary. As he looked back, he paid his tribute "to the [pastoral] calling, firm in the conviction that it offers greater opportunities for both moral adventure and social usefulness than any other calling if it is entered with open eyes and a consciousness of the hazards to virtue which lurk in it." Rarely later did he find open-eyed clerics. Most of them were wrapped in the illusions which he knew could come to people in contexts of mutual concern, responsibility, and love.[32]

Only rarely would he take pains to comment later on the intuitive and inherited wisdom and faithfulness of lay people, though he gave signs of an awareness of their qualities. In the *Christian Century* in 1934 he commented that "sometimes a healthy realism among laymen breaks through the illusions created by superficial moral preaching." Over against Christian idealists who "preach the law of love but forget that they . . . are involved in the violation of that law," he was "persuaded to thank God . . . that the common people maintain a degree of 'common sense,' that they preserve an uncorrupted ability to react against injustice and the cruelty of racial bigotry."[33] These

[31] *EAC*, pp. 12–14.

[32] *LNTC*, pp. 128, 74, 18.

[33] *Love and Justice: Selections from the Shorter Writings of Reinhold Niebuhr*, ed. D. B. Robertson (Philadelphia: Westminster Press, 1957), p. 42 (hereinafter cited as *LJ*).

compliments were rare, and they appeared almost exclusively when he wanted to make a point of lay realism over against clerical idealist folly.

Students of collective behavior in religion almost always preoccupy themselves with a study of ritual. Niebuhr was apparently only marginally interested in the esthetic and liturgical sides of religion, but he, too, did not underestimate the power of ritual. The editor of *Essays in Applied Christianity*, with compensatory vigor, reproduced eight essays on "The Weakness of Common Worship in American Protestantism." There Niebuhr commented on cathedral services, sermons and liturgy, and even architecture. His observer's eye was keen; most of what he saw in the Protestant churches reflected esthetic poverty, banality, and the separation of contemporaries from meaningful traditions: "There is a crying need for liturgical reform in American Protestantism." But that reform could not come if the evangelical churches merely aped the external estheticism of the liturgical churches. It would grow only out of a reevaluation of the whole meaning of worship. To make his case, Niebuhr discussed every nuance of typical church services.[34]

Burial rites play a major part in phenomenological treatments of religion; Niebuhr kept his eyes open. In Detroit he spoke well of the fact that Protestant funeral services took some cognizance of the "peculiar circumstances of a great sorrow" but were usually given to banalities and sentimentalities. "Religion is poetry. The truth in the poetry is vivified by adequate poetic symbols and is therefore more convincing than the poor prose with which the average preacher must attempt to grasp the ineffable." Both were superior to the generalized cultural burial rites parodied by Evelyn Waugh in *The Loved One*. Modern bourgeois culture's "effort to rob death of its sting by the perfection of appointments for coffin, grave and cemetery in funeral rites" was pathetic and perilous.[35]

Niebuhr often looked beyond the conventional churches; he knew that many of the churches went in "for vaudeville programs and . . . hip-hip-hooray" types of worship, with the "vulgarities of the stunt preacher." All this occurred in order for practitioners to compete for clienteles, especially among Methodists and Baptists, the large white denominations. He criticized Protestants who made churchgoing a

---

[34] *EAC*, pp. 29–66, esp. pp. 29 ff., 48, 52 ff., 58.
[35] *LNTC*, p. 50; *Faith and History: A Comparison of Christian and Modern Views of History* (New York: Charles Scribner's Sons, 1949), p. 156 (hereinafter cited as *FH*).

matter of moral heroism, a positive duty. He could question the idea that "a formless service is more spontaneous and therefore more religious than a formal one." He was critical of some church leaders' need to rely on pomp, garb, and paraphernalia to create a sense of awe for their office, but he never lost interest in the question of symbolism and garb. It was natural that he would deal with these topics most when he was charged with leading worship, but as a regular preacher and worshiper he never lost interest. "Ivory tower"—if this means the academy away from the church—was never the locale for Niebuhr's ruminations.[36]

RELIGIOUS BEHAVIOR IN SOCIAL CLASSES

Niebuhr made clear, however, that ritual, worship, liturgy, devotionalism, and esthetics would no more be the fundamental tests of modern religion than would its intellectuality. The test would be ethical, and his behavioral observation concentrated massively on that sphere. There his disappointment and disgust showed more frequently. He knew that while many Americans would not join in denunciation of organized religion, "there are very many who ignore the church as a force for social amelioration."[37]

His observation was routinely and rigidly socioeconomic in outlook. Niebuhr, a man in quest of an American proletariat—who despaired of finding one or seeing it form[38]—devoted surprisingly little attention to the lower-class churches, the forces of the dispossessed. Richard Niebuhr had given two chapters of his book on *The Social Sources of Denominationalism* to "the churches of the disinherited";[39] Reinhold made only cursory reference to the social dynamics of these. He treated the black churches almost only in contexts where he was chastising whites for discrimination. The churches of the Appalachian poor, the white slum dwellers, the Roman Catholic bottom-rung immigrants—all these were treated with passing reference, little curiosity, and little detailed knowledge. The sectarian and immigrant churches were not made up of a proletariat but of a set of people on the way toward middle-class vulgarization.

Niebuhr was almost determinist and mechanistic on one point. He tended to see the American experience as one in which sooner or later

---

[36] *LNTC*, pp. 162, 196, 82, 150–51.
[37] *DCNR*, p. 36.
[38] *REE*, p. 78.
[39] H. Richard Niebuhr, chaps. 2, 3.

almost everyone would be drawn as if by a magnet toward middle-class or bourgeois attitudes. It mattered little whether people came up from the ranks of the disinherited, from the late-arriving immigrant boats, or out of the segregated ex-slave churches. Somehow there would be eventual inevitable vulgarization and bourgeoisification, almost as if by a law of history. Here the determinist character of Niebuhr's observation was most patent. The "sect" churches he thought had been born honest, but in their conquest of the frontier they lost immediacy and mobility and became dominant, respectable, only vestigially charismatic. They secularized faith and let it lead to mere pursuit of worldly ends and sentimentality.[40]

The immigrant churches met similar fates. They became exclusive and guarded the immigrant against anomic urban culture. But what began as refuges from secular culture also served as a "resource for the uninhibited pursuits of essentially secular ends of life."[41] Churches became interesting to Niebuhr when they acquired middle-class semisecular status and were exposed to pluralist society.

THE CONSERVATIVE MIDDLE CLASSES

Niebuhr tended to classify middle-class religion—and here Protestantism interested him most consistently—along two lines. One was the semievangelical conservative religion of the American way of life, which was probably the majority pattern. Niebuhr needed the churches of this type for a discussion of normative American religion. They showed how pious citizens behave unless someone tampers with their patterns—as liberals were wont to do.

While his earlier works reflected an almost simplistic Marxian bias against the bourgeoisie, he softened criticism later and treated it ironically. In *The Irony of American History* he could even say that "the fluidity of the American class structure is . . . a gift of providence, being the consequence of a constantly expanding economy." This good fortune was sometimes "transmuted into social virtue" insofar as it left the worker free of social resentment and permitted the privileged classes to be less intransigent than had been their European counterparts in resistance to the rising classes. But when religious sanctions

---

[40] *Pious and Secular America* (New York: Charles Scribner's Sons, 1958), pp. 7–8 (hereinafter cited as *PSA*).

[41] Ibid., p. 11; see *DCNR*, pp. 98 ff.

were combined with this way of life, Niebuhr was rarely so affirmative. In one case he did say that the middle class along with workers "have been significant bearers of justice in history" and "would have been, and would be, more perfect instruments of justice if they had not been tempted to regard themselves as the final judges and the final redeemers of history." In practice, he studied this messianism more than the bearing of justice.[42]

By 1950–51 he saw that "the alliance between Protestant pietism and political reaction" was achieving a new triumph. The middle-class religionists' churches used economic individualism to forge the religion of "the American way of life." Sectarian Christianity was thus vulgarized. "The problems of [these] sects are more important because they represent the dominant force in American Protestantism. Perhaps they are also intrinsically more important. The church lives in conscious compromise with the world. The vitiated sect lives in unconscious compromise with the world. The first attitude may lead to premature defeatism. The second leads to sentimentality and self-deception."[43] "Unconscious compromise" fell into the scope of Niebuhr as an observer of collective behavior.

If agrarian classes had been the stronghold of religion, "the life of the middle classes of the city" was becoming the new locus. The middle classes are religious, the young Niebuhr had written, "because they are comparatively unconscious of their responsibility for society's sins and comparatively untouched by the evil consequences of an unethical civilization." So they may indulge hypocritically in a religion which creates respectability and self-respect.[44]

Niebuhr had least use for the fashionable bourgeois preachers, the "false prophets of our day" who "speak of our bourgeois civilisation as a 'Christian' civilisation." Bourgeois churches transmuted the idea of history into the Kingdom of God. The fashionable false prophets would almost always win favor. "There are a large number of eager young radical preachers in American Protestant churches who are engaged in the business of trying to make proletarians out of their middle-class church members." He knew American behavior. "It is a futile task." Surely "every common-sense realist, not to speak of religious realists, must know that masses of men, even when they are in Christian churches, move by interest" (1934). The bourgeois church

---

[42] *IAH*, p. 103; *DST*, p. 19.
[43] *EAC*, pp. 102, 41.
[44] *DCNR*, pp. 27–28.

exists to "sanctify power and privilege as it exists in the modern world."[45]

Despite its corruption, Niebuhr did not wish to see the middle-class church abandoned. Indeed, the prophet should concentrate there "because the church has the ear of these classes to a greater degree than that of the disinherited" and also because change in this class could be most significant.[46] In *Pious and Secular America* Niebuhr took a synoptic view of the problem. He agreed with Tocqueville, who a century earlier had noted the highly pragmatic character of American evangelical preachers. They moved from "eternal felicity" to the pursuit of worldly ends in their gospel. As a result, "It becomes apparent that we are more religious and more secular than any other nation, not by accident, but by the effect of definitely ascertainable historic causes peculiar to the American experience." "Piety has not essentially challenged . . . [the] vulgarity or futility." The result was "our gadget-filled paradise suspended in a hell of international insecurity." Foreign visitors were confused to find secular America "more religious in the devotion of a greater percentage of the population to the religious institutions which, contrary to expectation, grow rather than wither."[47]

Niebuhr knew that the sentimental and vulgarizing bond of religion and middle-class ideals was not wholly nonideological. In the nineteenth century the "survival of the fittest" concepts of Social Darwinism had served as an ideology when it was combined with "moribund Calvinism." More recently bourgeoisified Christianity had been corrupted by its bond with conservative doctrines. "Religious conservatism and fundamentalism" played into the hands of social conservatism. The movement called "Spiritual Mobilization," conducted by Dr. James Fifield of Los Angeles, was "one of the worst forms of religious rationalizations of a class viewpoint that we have had in American history." These formal ideological references were relatively rare in Niebuhr because they were unnecessary. Anyone with eyes could see: "There is not one church in a thousand where the moral problems of our industrial civilization are discussed with sufficient realism from the pulpit."[48]

Niebuhr's biblical realism, Puritan reminiscence, and critical

---

[45] *BT*, p. 107; *LJ*, pp. 44, 90.
[46] *LJ*, pp. 44–45.
[47] *PSA*, pp. 8, 11, 13, 31.
[48] *MNHC*, p. 64; *LJ*, pp. 111, 113; *PSA*, p. 20; *LJ*, p. 91 (1930).

Marxian viewpoint led him to blame individualism in economics for much of the corruption of this normative religious form. In practice, Americans were better than their individualist creed allowed in theory. Young men, "who have been assured that only the individual counts among us," had died for collective virtues on foreign battlefields. Here was "ironic refutation of our cherished creed" because the creed was too individualistic and optimistic. "It is necessary to be wiser than our creed if we would survive in the struggle against communism."[49]

Niebuhr contended that even middle-class churches could be better than their economic creed. Much of the popularity of the churches in the religious revival of the 1950s lay precisely in the fact that the individual could find his identity not over against an urban "crowd, gathered together by technics," but because some churches offered integral communities, where a person "lives in an environment of faith in which the vicissitudes of his existence are understood." Thus urbanness "has increased, rather than diminished, loyalty to the religious communities."[50] At the end of his career, Niebuhr even showed a rare awareness of the historical depths of this communitarian contribution that reached back to Jonathan Edwards in the eighteenth and Charles Grandison Finney in the nineteenth century. Both awakeners and awakenings "were productive of social as well as of individual creative commitments," and gave rise to antislavery and other social causes—even though people were eventually to lose heart in these causes.

The faults of this evangelicalism lay in its individualism and perfectionism.[51] Observing behavior based on these commitments was a regular Niebuhrian preoccupation. "Protestant pietistic individualism" became a frequently used phrase in his later works just as observations of it had been common in his earliest. This individualism led religious leaders to focus on personal petty vices rather than on great social evils. His first book underscored this: "In America, Protestantism with its individualism became a kind of spiritual sanctification of the peculiar interests and prejudices of the races and classes which dominated the industrial and commercial expansion of Western civilization." Ministers were tempted in "our great urban churches" to "become again the simple priests and chaplains of this American idolatry."[52]

[49] *IAH*, p. 10.
[50] *PSA*, p. 6.
[51] *MNHC*, pp. 122–23.
[52] *FP*, pp. 119–20; *LNTC*, p. 117; *DCNR*, p. 67; *LJ*, p. 97.

Niebuhr the prophet and theologian took his vision of bourgeois Christianity and called it to its biblical and, in the American instance, its Catholic and Puritan roots. "The social life of man" is "the source of common grace." To come to this understanding, "the adherent of religion must come to terms with the historic facts, that *in all collective behavior religious piety is likely to sanctify historical and contingent viewpoints*" (emphasis mine). Puritanism, he knew, worked both ways. Religiously it could bring the collective sphere into the orbit of God's judgment and common grace. Secularly it had transmuted a doctrine of providence and of the calling into economic individualism. Since New England days, "any grateful acceptance of God's uncovenanted mercies is easily corrupted from gratitude to self-congratulations if it is believed that providence represents not the grace of a divine power ... but rather that it represents particular divine acts directly correlated to particular human and historical situations." To Niebuhr it was clear that Americans characteristically acted self-congratulatorily.[53]

"The whole non-Lutheran Protestant world," which meant the American non-Catholic majority, was "indoctrinated with [the] puritan spirit." This "puritanism is a religious sublimation of the life of the middle classes." For the heroic spirit of puritanism declined "in those classes which it had lifted to power," and was "reborn in the lower middle classes," which it helped turn into successful classes. "The puritan heritage of America ... gives a clew to the paradox of our national life. It explains how we can be at the same time the most religious and the most materialistic of all modern nations."[54]

THE LIBERAL MIDDLE CLASSES

While the neo-orthodox Niebuhr was sometimes accused of being identified with conservative-pessimist Christianity because of his biblical concern and his restoration of the doctrine of original sin, no one ever accused him of being confused or bound up with pietist, individualist, evangelically orthodox, or fundamentalist churches. He showed that he was a prophet of biblical realism by turning most of his polemic attention against the churches in whose sphere he was located, the liberal minority in the essentially middle-class American context. He seemed to have despaired of fundamentalism; it was almost beyond redemption. The churches he served, the campuses he visited, the journals for which he wrote, the parties he advised, the seminarians he

[53] *MNHC*, pp. 120, 11; *IAH*, pp. 50.
[54] *DCNR*, pp. 102–3.

taught—all these were tinged with what he called liberalism. Their collective behavior patterns and their doctrines disturbed him most. He treated them nomothetically and stereotypically, rarely pointing to exceptions or citing individuals who transcended the boundaries he erected.

The first great work in which Niebuhr attacked the liberal middle-class churches was *An Interpretation of Christian Ethics*. He had repudiated that Social Gospel which had helped form him. The depression revealed the limits of the sentimental moral individualism and progressive optimism which had been the marks of the old liberal churches. Foreboding totalitarian powers in Europe further eluded their comprehensions. "The religion and ethics of the liberal church is dominated by the desire to prove to its generation that it does not share the anachronistic ethics or believe the incredible myths of orthodox religion." But, "in adjusting itself to the characteristic credos and prejudices of modernity, the liberal church has been in constant danger of obscuring what is distinctive in the Christian message and creative in Christian morality." Those lines pretty well delineate what might almost be called one of two separate churches in Niebuhr's observation. These churches cast a false aura of the absolute and transcendent ethic of Jesus around the "relative moral standards of a commercial age" and then capitulated to that age. They were too uncritically accommodated to modern culture, as the discrediting of that culture was progressively revealing.

Liberal Christianity was a religion of adjustment to the ethos of this age, a sacrifice of the Christian heritage through its destruction of "the sense of depth and the experience of tension" typical of profound religion. These churches also endorsed laissez faire economic patterns until too late. By overstressing love and cooperation in place of conflict and coercion he removed the grounds for the socializing of life. The Federal Council of Churches (FCC) the endorsement of the League of Nations, the predilections for pacifism—which Niebuhr had been deserting—all showed how compromising liberalism in practice had become. These criticisms were constant in Niebuhr's later works and became so familiar that they hardly deserve citation here. Here it need only be noted that while Niebuhr brought ideological assumptions to his observations, he was, indeed, an observer—and a consistent one—of liberalism's behavioral regularities.[55]

[55] *An Interpretation of Christian Ethics* (New York: Harper & Bros., 1935), pp. 15, 20, 22, 25, 186–87 (hereinafter cited as *ICE*).

Because of their blindness to tragedy in a warring world, he noted: "If the modern churches were to symbolize their true faith they would take the crucifix from their altars and substitute the three little monkeys who counsel men to 'speak no evil, hear no evil, see no evil.'" These churches close their eyes to suffering and "drug their conscience" so that they can make no significant distinctions between contending political forces. In order to make the point of the sentimental practice of liberal religion, Niebuhr even opened his mail for his readers and told of a parson who wanted to set "moral force" against Hitler's battalions. This was a "nice example of the sentimentalized form of Christianity which has engulfed our churches in America, and which has prompted them to dream of 'spiritualizing life' by abstracting spirit from matter, history, and life." [56]

The version of liberal Christianity that gave Niebuhr most problems was the Social Gospel. The embarrassment was evident when he was invited to give the Rauschenbusch lectures, dedicated to the foremost advocate of the liberal Social Gospel. Niebuhr hoped that his lectures were "an extension and an application to our own day of both the social realism and the loyalty ot the Christian faith" which characterized Walter Rauschenbusch, the brilliant founder and exponent of social Christianity. But throughout his career Niebuhr attacked the Social Gospel because its proponents "had . . . a faith which did not differ too grievously from the main outlines of the 'American dream.'" The Social Gospel displayed "a curious mixture of bourgeois prudence" with the pinnacle of grace, the message of the gospels. [57]

The final flaw in liberal religious practice was the almost consistent pacifism expressed in pre–World War II America. Liberal pacifism played into the hands of those who already had economic power, but it became more damaging when the demonic powers of Europe were underestimated by pacifists. Niebuhr's foils on this front were the FCC, where liberal churches were amassed, and the journal, *Christian Century*—with which he had been associated—which kept alive the progressive liberalism and optimism of the Social Gospel. Niebuhr's Christian realism needed a new outlet, and he helped form *Christianity and Crisis*. The FCC and the *Christian Century* were "completely divorced from all political realities" in their actions and attitudes toward Hitler. "Most of the neutrals of Europe to whose conscience the

---

[56] *Christianity and Power Politics* (New York: Charles Scribner's Sons, 1940), p. 109 (hereinafter cited as *CPP*); *CRPP*, p. 109; *CPP*, p. 173.

[57] *ICE*, p. 7; Kegley and Bretall, p. 13; *CRPP*, 163.

Christian Century pointed were destroyed while it was holding them up as glorious examples."[58]

While Niebuhr saw pacifism as an absolutist creed, he criticized it chiefly as a practical pattern born of a bad conscience over American hysteria in World War I and "the national fear of being involved in the war." The pacifists refused to look at the horrible consequences of tyranny. Here, as so often, Niebuhr looked at the behavior of the American and particularly the liberal churches. "The Christian Church in America has never been upon a lower level of spiritual insight and moral sensitivity than in this tragic age of world conflict. Living in a suffering world, with its ears assailed by the cries of the miserable victims of tyranny and conflict, it has chosen to identify the slogan Keep America out of the War with the Christian gospel."[59]

THE CONDUCT OF NATION AND TRIBE

Niebuhr moved progressively away from seeing the churches as the repository of religious conviction and practice in America. He turned more and more to the need for seeing the nation itself in this role, though without denying the special custodial responsibilities of the Christian believing community. In this turn, Niebuhr began to combine in his person and vocation the once separate strands of past American public theology. We have seen Edwards, Bushnell, and Rauschenbusch typically using the covenanted religious community as a base for public action, while Franklin (or Jefferson), Lincoln, Wilson, and their kind were essentially public political figures who saw a kind of ecclesiastical dimension in national life. Niebuhr kept the tension between the two spheres, but also brought them dialectically into creative interplay and occasional fusion. He will be remembered more for his grasp of the irony of pious and secular American history than for any contributions to the sociology of religion.

While Niebuhr treated the church somewhat statically and stereotypically, he looked at the nation more dynamically. It seemed to be less of a finished product, more open to having its attitudes and practical patterns subjected to radical change. His later contacts were more with national than ecclesiastical figures: George Kennan, Dean Acheson, Arthur Schlesinger, Jr., Hans Morgenthau, Walter Lippmann, and James Reston make more of their debt to him than did ecumenical

[58] *ICE*, pp. 58–59; *CPP*, pp. 42–45.
[59] *CPP*, pp. 75–78, 32.

statesmen who, of course, also fell under his influence. Perhaps most revelatory of Niebuhr's final locale or situation was his designation of Abraham Lincoln and not a church leader as "America's greatest theologian."[60] His writings show a general agreement with the contention of his long-time colleague, Paul Tillich, that religion is the soul of culture and culture the form of religion, and he saw America as a problematic concretization of a spiritual reality.

Widely read in American sources he operated basically out of pragmatic considerations and day-to-day observations. With his coauthor, historian Alan Heimert, he opened a work on the American character with lines which summarize my essay: "The character of both nations and individuals may be defined as a pattern of consistent behavior, created on the one hand by an original ethnic, geographic and cultural endowment, and on the other hand by the vicissitudes of history, which shape and reshape, purify, corrupt and transmute this endowment."[61] Niebuhr was aware of the particularity of this American history, but spoke critically of representatives of "our nominalistic culture" who were "intent upon finding specific causes for general tendencies" and who ascribed to American life certain universal human tendencies.[62]

The nation was not an autonomous generator of valid religious values; in the case of America, the Christian message had been especially determining. As had all the public theologians before him, Niebuhr wanted the churches to see "positively our task to present the Gospel of redemption in Christ to nations as well as to individuals." The church also had to "recognize that there are sensitive secular elements within modern nations, who, though they deny the reality of a divine judgment, are nevertheless frequently more aware of the perils of national pride than many members of the Church."[63]

As soon as Niebuhr mentioned national religiosity he would find it necessary to speak of the temptations of hybris and to idolatry. American citizens characteristically behaved idolatrously, and churches were little check against their tendency. "The god of American religion (the so-called 'American dream') is an American god." "Nowhere is the temptation to idolatry greater than in national life." "The idolatrous devotion to the 'American way of life' grows at a tremendous

[60] Quoted by June Bingham, *Courage to Change: An Introduction to the Life and Thought of Reinhold Niebuhr* (New York: Charles Scribner's Sons, 1961), p. 310.

[61] *NSC*, p. 7.

[62] *CRPP*, p. 9.

[63] Ibid., p. 111; *DST*, p. 30.

pace." Niebuhr used the business community and its devotion to the "free enterprise system" to demonstrate the point.[64]

How would idolatrous practices be countered? From two fronts. "There is no conceivable society in which the pride of the community and the arrogance of its oligarchs must not be resisted. It is possible to offer this resistance at times in the name of some minority interest." For example, religious, ethnic, and economic subcommunities "both enriched and imperiled the life of the community." "But the final resistance must come from the community which knows and worships a God, to whom all nations are subject."[65]

Americans acted not only idolatrously but also innocently, as if their nation were exempt from temptations of power and pride. Drawing on century-old observations of conduct by Tocqueville, Niebuhr commented that while every nation had an innocent and self-appreciative concept, "our version is that our nation turned its back upon the vices of Europe and made a new beginning." Because of the conflict between American ideals and realities, Niebuhr resorted to the basic category of irony to interpret national life. "Irony ... prompts some laughter and a nod of comprehension beyond the laughter; for irony involves comic absurdities which cease to be altogether absurd when fully understood. Our age is involved in irony because so many dreams of our nation have been so cruelly refuted by history." For dealing with this irony not a churchman, but President Abraham Lincoln, was the model interpreter and theologian. "Lincoln's awareness of the element of pretense in the idealism of both sides was rooted in his confidence in an overarching providence whose purposes partly contradicted and were yet not irrelevant to the moral issues of the conflict."[66]

In *Beyond Tragedy* Niebuhr quoted Stephen Vincent Benet putting words into the mouth of Lincoln—words which underscored the concern for the churches' behavior patterns in American life:

> They come to me and talk about God's will
> In righteous deputations and platoons,
> Day after day, laymen and ministers.
> ... God's will is those poor coloured fellows' will,
> It is the will of the Chicago churches,

---

[64] *BT*, pp. 53, 85; *LJ*, pp. 94–95.
[65] *BT*, p. 86; *CLCD*, p. 124; *BT*, p. 86.
[66] *IAH*, pp. 78, 7, 171.

It is this man's and his worst enemy's.
But all of them are sure they know God's will.
I am the only man who does not know it.[67]

The nation stood as the powerful midpoint between the ethnic, religious, and economic subcommunities and the international community; for Niebuhr, it deserved most attention, but not in isolation. He was highly aware of region, of differences in North and South so far as race, religion, and nationalism were concerned. He even spoke of "the geography of morals," noting how different the church practices of similar denominations were in different regions.[68]

Niebuhr watched ethnic and racial subcommunities in action and was ambivalent. On one hand, their assertions of particularity could be a matter of tribal pride. "The chief source of man's inhumanity to man seems to be the tribal limits of his sense of obligation to other men." "America, which has prided itself on being the 'melting pot' of many ethnic groups" was as late as the 1960s still trying to rid itself of tribalism that antedated the Civil War. Language, class, and religion joined race to create tribal distinctions. On the other hand, as dangerous as tribalism was, Niebuhr also saw virtues in subcommunities. In reference to the Jewish community he argued that the attempt to "solve the problem of the particularity of a race by a cultural or religious universalism" was false and destructive. He was critical of both "premature universalism" and a "conscious or unconscious ethnic imperialism." He had long been aware that integrationist models and tendencies toward universalism usually resulted from one's tendency "to make his own standards the final norms of existence and to judge others for failure to conform to them."[69]

The appreciation of the *plures* that interacted in the American *unum* resulted in part, he said, from the influence of his wife Ursula, who taught at Barnard College. She was "responsible for modifying my various forms of provincialism and homiletical polemics." Once again, his viewpoint was born of situation—or, at least, his wife's situation and circumstance. In his final retrospect he also credited Detroit Judaism for having made early and substantial contributions to his sense of justice born of particular subcommunities' witness. American

[67] Stephen Vincent Benet, *John Brown's Body* (New York: Farrar & Rinehart, 1928), p. 213; cited in *BT*, pp. 66–67.
[68] *MMIS*, p. 119; *The Structure of Nations and Empires* (New York: Charles Scribner's Sons., 1959), pp. 214–15 (hereinafter cited as *SNE*); *LNTC*, p. 190.
[69] *MNHC*, pp. 84–87; *LJ*, p. 127; *CLCD*, p. 140.

Christians too often practiced "provisional tolerance" awaiting Jewish assimilation—and the end of Jewish identity and contribution. So awed was he by the realism and tenacity of America's Jews that he sometimes exempted them from the searching criticism he gave Christians. And Roman Catholics he eventually also viewed favorably from a distance, overestimating the degree to which their church temporarily spared them middle-class vulgarization and individual economic striving. Yet it was characteristic of him that he should train his eye and reserve his judgment for his own community. "Even in our nation, priding itself on its melting pot, the Protestant faith is undoubtedly an instrument of pride and cohesion for the North European or 'Nordic' groups, as distinguished from the Slavs and the Latins. Every Protestant denomination has some particular ethnic or historical particularity." This racial and even racist base of Protestant cohesion and conduct came to be reported on as commonplace in the 1970s, but was a rare observation in 1958 when Niebuhr made it. Even in his first book he could observe that "Orthodox Protestantism is intimately related to this day with Nordicism, with the racial arrogance of north European peoples."[70]

Nowhere did the problem of interpreting America as a spiritual reality present more problems for a synoptic thinker like Niebuhr than in the case of the majority's treatment of segregated blacks. Here, again, behavior was determining. "The churches, as Negro Christians long ago ruefully admitted, have been the most segregated communities in the ... nation." This has been the negative by-product of one of the genuine achievements of the sectarian church in our nation: "the creation of integral communities on the level of local congregations," where "chumminess" invalidated the universal principle at the heart of the gospel.

Niebuhr's appreciation of Judaism and Catholicism was born of practical, and not dogmatic, awareness of their ability to transcend some of these circumstances. He even apologized to members of these religious groups, hoping they would "not be too shocked by the wholly pragmatic sources of my appreciations."[71]

Niebuhr's public theology not only related the nation to the tribe but also to supernation or internationalism. He was observant of the historical and not simply psychologically determining roots of national difference. The culturally relativist anthropologists lacked an "appre-

[70] *MNHC*, pp. 28, 17; see also *PSA*, pp. 90 ff., 88, 111; *DCNR*, p. 70.
[71] *PSA*, p. 82; *MNHC*, p. 20.

ciation of the genuinely historical differences" between these national cultures. German problems could not be explained "as the consequence of defects in the toilet training." [72] One had to study the whole complex context of national conduct in historical lineages. It is not necessary here to detail Niebuhr's concepts of world community, the need for American expressions of responsibility, or his desire to see his nation purged of illusionistic idealism vis-à-vis other nations. At this point reference is in place only to his regard for national differences, so far as conduct and interest as well as ideology are concerned.

If Niebuhr was responsive to what some have come to call a civil religion, this awareness was born of his frustration over the limits of what particular churches could achieve. Never was it uncritical or short of prophetic; his every appreciation was tinged with irony and marked by realism. And his national concerns had an ecumenical dimension: if God was somehow seen to be the transcendent reference for interpreting the life of the American people he was not less related to other nations and communities.

For all the limits in Niebuhr's observation and despite some hidden ideological biases and tendencies to stereotype, he joined in his person the two main approaches to public theology in America. He took the behavior of his people and, reflecting on it in the light of biblical, historical, and philosophical positions, offered the ensuing generation a paradigm for a public theology, a model which his successors have only begun to develop and realize.

[72] *SDH*, p. 142.

Reinhold Niebuhr's Theology of History

Langdon Gilkey

Since Reinhold Niebuhr conceived his theological interpretation of history some three decades ago, a great deal has changed in the climate of both the sociopolitical and the theological worlds. The defense of democratic culture against fascism as the dominant historical concern of theologians has been replaced by the critique of Western capitalistic and imperialistic culture by those many groups oppressed by it. Communism has ceased to represent a monolithic, totalitarian structure—both in its Stalinist structural embodiment and in its orthodox theory—and become a variegated and often impressively creative social pattern with a number of divergent theoretical interpretations. Above all, creative movements of "liberation," among the blacks, among women, and among the nations of the Third World, have appeared, demanding new theological interpretation, legitimation, and criticism and, in their drive toward a more human future, apparently requiring a different sort of interpretation of history than any of the neoorthodoxies proffered. In response to this new historical situation there have also appeared a wide variety of "theologies of liberation," eschatological in emphasis and politically radical in their implications, associated with the names of Pannenberg, Moltmann, Metz, Alvez, Gutierrez, and Braaten, among others. Deliberately all of these men have constructed theology on a quite different dogmatic or doctrinal basis than did either their neoorthodox Protestant or their Catholic predecessors, and they have given that theology a quite different orientation to the human situation, namely, one directed at the social structures within which men and women exist, at history, rather than at their inward, private states of consciousness or "self-understanding," at individual existence and personal decisions. With this change of both political and theological climate the theology and political ethic of Niebuhr have been roundly criticized: as essentially pragmatic rather than utopian and so compromising to a fault; as "liberal" in social values and political philosophy (if not in theology) and so in concrete fact a conservative apologia for American culture; as so "realistic" as to be unable to bring judgment on present social evils; as pessimistic vis-à-vis the social future and so enervating politically; as concerned with personal reconciliation rather than revolutionary or even reformist social change—and so ironically in the end blessing rather than challenging the status quo. If the developmentalism of Protestant liberalism was for the early Niebuhr a theological rationalization of bourgeois American culture because of its optimism, then for his Third World and New Left critics Niebuhr's pragmatic relativism and neoorthodox realism provided through its pessimism an even more effective (because more dialectical and so subtle) defense of that same culture.

Now, although to be sure Niebuhr's interpretation of history reflected the neoorthodox emphasis on transcendence and reconciliation, and so on inner, "existential" repentance, humility, and trust, still it is undeniable that his theology never became exclusively private or inward as much of neoorthodoxy did. Even at the height of his theological and so "neoorthodox" concerns, he could say that the Gospel provides an interpretation of history as well as of individual existence; [1] that Christ is the principle for the meaning of the whole of human history; [2] that sin is largely social and collective in form; [3] that the main point of Christian faith and of sound theology is as a creative framework for social and political decisions and action; and that therefore one main criterion of theological validity is not only an interpretation's adequacy to the "facts" of social experience and to the biblical symbolism but even more its effectiveness in initiating, in fact requiring, creative and transformative political action for larger justice, equality, and peace. [4] The theological meaning of biblical and Christian symbols represented for him primarily an ethical meaning, as opposed to an

[1] See, e.g., *Faith and History* (New York: Charles Scribner's Sons, 1949), pp. 20 ff. (hereafter cited as *FH*); *The Nature and Destiny of Man*, 2 vols. (New York: Charles Scribner's Sons, 1941, 1943), 2:5, 35 ff. (hereafter cited as *ND*).

[2] *ND*, 2:5; *FH*, p. 26.

[3] His writings are replete with examples of this point (see esp. *Moral Man and Immoral Society* [New York: Charles Scribner's Sons, 1932] and *Reflections on the End of an Era* [New York: Charles Scribner's Sons, 1934]). For my point that this is also true in his "theological" writings, see *ND*, vol. 1, the examples of sin as pride in chap. 7; chap. 8, pts. 1, 2; and the illustration of "original sin" in terms of Nazism in chap. 9.

[4] See, e.g., *The Interpretation of Christian Ethics* (New York: Harper & Bros., 1935), chaps. 5, 6.

ontological or even an experiential meaning; and, as is clear from all his major theological works as well as his political and social writings, ethics meant for him social and political ethics. That is, when he tried to say what a symbol meant, he usually explicated it as, on the one hand, a guard against collective pride and so political injustice and, on the other, a lure and ground for communal and so political transformation.

Thus, unlike that of Bultmann and Barth, Niebuhr's theology represents only a "half-hearted" existentialist neoorthodoxy. Instead of using Reformation and existentialist categories exclusively to interpret man's inner situation and to provide a theological framework for his individual decisions, Niebuhr used them to interpret social and communal, "objective," history, and to provide a framework for Christian political decisions. As much as his present eschatological critics, therefore, his was a political and not a private, interiorized theology, a theology whose goal was creative *praxis*, not contemplative reflection—and yet, in contrast to those critics, it was in the end a theology of reconciliation through the Atonement and so of justification, rather than one of eschatological promise and fulfillment in a historical Kingdom. Our questions in this essay are, then: (1) what sort of view of history and its social possibilities does this Reformation or neo-orthodox framework provide in Niebuhr's hands (I shall concentrate on his theology of history rather than on his pragmatic political ethic; happily, as I have just discovered, the latter is the subject of Prof. Shinn's article in this issue); (2) how does this theological interpretation of history differ from the view of history and its possibilities of the eschatological theologies of liberation; and (3) what can be said, in the present concern for the humanization of our social world, for this perspective on the future? Since this is an essay on Niebuhr's views, I shall concentrate on his view of history and not on that of the contemporary eschatologists; however, I shall try to describe his thought always in juxtaposition to theirs so as to make visible how these very different theological structures view a common subject, namely, history and its possibilities for the social and political future.

* * *

At the start a very brief summary of the theological anatomy of the eschatological political theologies is necessary. Clearly this will be inadequate and of necessity undocumented, and so it will miss many important nuances of difference among potent thinkers. I hope that it is accurate enough to provide a valid and meaningful contrast to Niebuhr's thought.

1) For all of them eschatology is the key to theology; that is, eschatology is that symbol or set of symbols which define and elucidate all other Christian symbols. Even more important, eschatology is or points to the future. It has a temporal locus and reference, to "what is to come," to what "lies ahead," to the "new" that is to appear in future time and in future history. The fundamental dialectic in these theologies is, therefore, temporal, one between two temporal ages: a sinful and suffering past and present, on the one hand, and the new future of God on the other. This dialectic is thus reminiscent of the progressivist view of history, for which the future is also the realm of redemption; the difference is that here the future does not arise out of the past as in developmentalism but the reverse, each present arising out of the impingement on it of its future. (2) Man is understood as man primarily in relation to the future. Openness to the future and hope for it define his self-transcendence and his freedom; they are therefore the qualities that make him human and are in turn creative of his historicity. Correspondingly, his perfection is a life lived in openness, hope, commitment, and action in relation to the promised new that is to come. (3) God also is understood in terms of the category of the future: not as at the beginning, or as "above" (both of which bless what is), but as "ahead," as the God who is coming, and who, in negating what has been and is, will usher in the new. The fullness of God's being is future; his power works on the present from the future (and has so worked on every present); his intentions are to create a new future; and his promises refer to the final fulfillment of history in the future when his sovereignty and rule will be manifest in the realized kingdom. He is the power of the future who "masters every present," and whose own redemptive future is the ultimate future of every contingent present. (4) Human sin is equivalent, therefore, to devotion to past and present, bondage to what has been, and closedness to the new that is approaching—and so defiance of God who represents this new future. The social correlates of sin, the major sources of "evil" and so of massive suffering in history, are the structures, political and economic, that survive in the present from the past. (5) Christian revelation is not the present self-communication of God to our inward spirits but his promises concerning the future. Thus the role of Christ as revealer is primarily proleptic, he who (especially in his Resurrection) is the earnest and sign of what is to come, and, who, especially in the Catholic forms of this theology, through his incarnation empowers his community in its task to realize the new future of the world. (6)

Salvation, therefore, is the ultimate sociohistorical future which is the Kingdom (this *is* God, as Pannenberg puts it, when God's power and rule, and so his being, are manifest), a kingdom in history as history's fulfillment, a kingdom of justice, love, and true humanity. It is this "realized eschatology" in the future that is the meaning of history and its fulfillment—though in all, and most explicitly in Pannenberg, that realization extends also beyond the barrier of death. Even from this truncated—but I hope not too inaccurate—description, it can be seen how this theology, as promised, is dominated by futurist eschatology, however modernized the form of that futurism may be, and how, in its promise of a new historical world in the future, it undeniably provides a religious and theological ground for revolutionary movements of liberation.

When one turns from this theological "world" to that of Niebuhr, one encounters an entirely different structure or anatomy of thought, a vastly different way of understanding man, sin, history, God, revelation, redemption, and so the possibilities of the future. Our task in the remainder of this essay is to disclose the anatomy of this different theology, to see what comments Niebuhr's view might suggest vis-à-vis the eschatological political theologies, and so why his thought may be of continuing concern to theologians interested in politics and history.

1. The fundamental dialectic in Niebuhr's thought is not that between present and future, a temporal dialectic, but that between transcendence and creatureliness, between eternity and time (in his earlier works), between God and world. This is a *vertical* dialectic expressive of the relatedness to and impingement upon every present (*not* by its future) by the transcendent "vertically" beyond and yet vertically related to past, present, *and* future. Although temporality and the future—and openness to them—are important categories in Niebuhr's understanding, they by no means define the other symbols. It is the vertical dialectic that is in that sense definitive, the "model" with which every other symbol is discussed and elaborated from creation through anthropology, revelation, Christology, and grace to eschatology. Thus while eschatology has a significant role in Niebuhr's theology, his theology is not properly called "eschatological"—unless, as for example in Barth and Bultmann, that symbol in turn is itself defined in terms of the vertical dialectic.

Let us take some familiar examples of the vertical dialectic as definitive for Niebuhr's thought. As is well known, man is here defined as at once creature and image of God, as finite, partial, temporal, fragmentary, contingent, and "subject to nature's and history's necessities," and yet self-transcendent, as able to stand "beyond" his world, his time, his society, his self—and so to find his limits, identity, place, individuality, task, genuine community and security only in God.[5] Here man so to speak rises vertically from a finite and particular base, and *thus* is he man; free to break and then reshape the forms of natural instinct (the harmonies of nature), the orders of social cohesion and custom (the harmonies of society), and the intellectual order of norms and of thought (the harmonies of reason). It is this vertical ascent that distinguishes human history from nature, since on it human creativity and so the new in history are dependent;[6] it is this that creates man's historical consciousness (note that memory of the past is as important for Niebuhr as is anticipation of the future in man's consciousness of history).[7] It is man's transcendence over every structure in relating to God's will that is the basis for the religious (or prophetic) challenge to all political structures—not the fact that they are all "questionable" because of man's transcendence into a new future, as in the theologies of the eschatologists. Revelation, in turn, is the self-communication of the transcendent God (the correlate of man's self-transcendence), of his power, purposes, and love to self-transcendent man:[8] in "general" revelation as source and ground, and as call and judgment; in "special" revelation as obligation and judgment, and above all as mercy. The inner response to revelation is faith or trust, the appropriate qualification of such a self-transcendent creature in direct personal relation to his source, ruler, and end, namely, that man's freedom and so his total existence be centered in the transcendent purposes and harmony of God's providential will and not in his own.[9] As the centrally determining relation of self-transcendent creature to creator, anchoring man's security and freedom in

---

[5] E.g., *ND*, 1:14, 124–25, 152 ff., 167 ff.

[6] *ND*, 1:26; 2:1.

[7] *FH*, pp. 19–20.

[8] *ND*, 1:126–37.

[9] *ND*, 1:168, 183, 251–53, 271, 289; *FH*, pp. 36–37, 57. It is important to note that wherever he speaks of *faith*, Niebuhr relates this, as the conquest of anxiety, to trust in *providence*, God's work within the course of history and so in the *immediate future*—rather than to promises about the end, in relation to the *ultimate* future. This is not to deny that for Niebuhr Christ is central in defining God's providential will and so the object of faith; it is merely to say that the will so defined and related to in faith as *trust* is the providential will of God within history and not his eschatological will for the end or culmination of history.

God's providence, faith is the principle of man's perfection and the possibility of his creativity in the future, that is, of renewal of life and of new possibility through finding his security not in finite self but in God's providential sovereignty. Through vertical relation to God in faith, man can face without destructive anxiety the contingencies of the future—an important difference from the eschatologists, for whom the relation of faith is only to the promises through which man in turn relates in hope to the God of the future! Thus while in the latter faith as a relation to the promises (and not directly to God) is subordinate to hope, which *is* the relation to the God of the future, in Niebuhr's theology faith is the relation to the transcendent God of the present, and so hope is one form of faith vis-à-vis the anxieties of the future.[10]

For Niebuhr, then, the essence of biblical revelation—as manifested first in the prophets—is the appearance of this "Word" of transcendence impinging, so to speak, from above on every present, on the ambiguous world of history. The transcendence of that Word over individual and collective alike is first symbolized in the covenant (not in future promise) in which Israel is chosen;[11] and it is realized further in the prophetic word of judgment on Israel's pride[12]—leaving open still the question of the meaning of history if even the "chosen" are thus judged[13] (note on what different principles the prophetic word is completed in Christ in the two theologies!). As is already evident, God is understood according to the vertical dialectic:[14] transcendent to and yet related with our creaturely being in creation, transcendent to and yet related with our freedom and conscience in our humanity, and transcendent to and yet related with our sinful behavior in judgment and redemption. This theme of God's dialectical transcendence and yet relatedness, as Creator, Judge, and Redeemer—always vertically impinging on our present though defined by events in the past—is elaborated with increasing sharpness, culminating in the masterful

---

[10] *ND*, 1:271, 289.

[11] *FH*, pp. 24, 102–4; *ND*, 1:137.

[12] *ND*, 1:214; 2:25.

[13] *ND*, 2:27–31.

[14] *ND*, 1:126 ff.; *FH*, 102 ff. Note in these examples (especially that in *FH*) of the "transcendence and yet relatedness of God" that when Niebuhr explicates the meaning of this transcendence and yet relatedness, it is not the ontological meaning of such a concept that concerns him, but the ethical and political meanings; i.e., a relation to transcendence answers the question of how a group can find meaning in its common life without making itself the center of history and so doing injustice to others.

picture of the *agape* of God as the "final pinnacle" of the divine transcendence of mercy over divine law and yet relatedness through loving acceptance.[15]

If in this way this vertical dialectic is central throughout Niebuhr's theology in place of the temporal dialectic of the eschatologists, clearly for him history will have a quite different sort of meaning. Here past and future do not form the major antitheses of theology, with the result that for Niebuhr the historical future cannot and will not be identical with redemption or final fulfillment. Rather, the transcendent God impinging on all of history and yet never identical with any portion of it is the principle of historical meaning. Theologically, therefore, history in its fundamental character is all of one piece, not separated into two aeons; the dialectic is vertical, not horizontal and temporal. Thus God's "final" self-communication in history points for Niebuhr to the *disclosure* of history's meaning in Jesus Christ, not, as for the eschatologist, to the *fulfillment* of history's meaning in the future Parousia, of which Jesus Christ is only the promise.[16] The meaning in history that is disclosed in Christ comes, therefore, from God's work in continuing history in relation to man's freedom, not from God's acts in the ultimate future. Here God's role as continuing creator, judge, providence, and redeemer in relation to man's being, his freedom, his sin, and his renewal gives meaning to history, not God's unequivocal sovereignty at the end. Such unequivocal sovereignty for Niebuhr would not be history any longer because it would no longer reflect man's creatureliness, his self-transcendence, and his continuing sin. In any case, let us note that contrary to the repeated arguments of the eschatologists, a vertical dialectic, the transcendent God "above" the moving moments of time, does not necessarily result in a private, inward, ahistorical theology.

Before I go on to elaborate the complex of themes in the last paragraph, it might be useful to see how Niebuhr views the concept of "man's openness to the future" in comparison to the eschatologists. As we saw, for the latter, openness to the future as opposed to bondage to the past represented the redemptive possibility of man, his perfection in history. For Niebuhr, in contrast, it represents the essential or ontological situation of man which thus sets the condition for his problems as much as it defines his perfection. For Niebuhr man as self-transcendent transcends his present temporal locus, both in being

[15] *ND*, 2:70–72, 92.
[16] *ND*, 2:35, 54–55, 67; *FH*, p. 139; *ND*, 1:132.

able to view his past in memory and to anticipate and imagine possibilities of all sorts for his future.[17] He is thus as spirit, says Niebuhr, aware (a) of his contingency in both nature and history—which means he is aware of contingent possibilities, positive and negative, creative and menacing, in his immediate future—and (b) of the infinite possibilities open to him in the future as free and self-determinative, aware that there are no easily discernible limits to what he is and so to what he may become in the future. He faces contingent possibilities as a creature and infinite possibilities as free spirit, and out of this dual "openness to the future" his anxiety is bred, the creative anxiety to exceed particular limits into new possibilities, and the destructive anxiety to secure himself amidst the menacing possibilities of his contingency. All of his actions reflect, and intermingle, these two implications of "openness to future possibilities" and so these two facets of anxiety.[18] And out of this situation of openness, essential to man as man—plus the "false interpretation of this situation"— arises not man's perfection or redemption but the possibility and the actuality of his fall, his sinful efforts to surpass his limits and thus to secure himself.[19] Man sins not because he is bound to his past—as really "bound to his past" he would for Niebuhr hardly be free enough to be man or to sin. He sins because he is *not* bound to his past, because he is open to the future and all of its possibilities, and so without faith and trust he is, as contingent, anxious *in* that openness and makes himself God, obscuring that contingency and finitude which were made unsupportable *by* that openness. Thus hope does not for Niebuhr "open" the future and so possibility—they are already open through man's essential freedom and so form the conditions of his sin. Faith rather makes that ineradicably open future with all its ambiguous possibilities bearable and thus itself is the sole ground of hope.[20] As is evident, the vertical dialectic gives an entirely different, and I suggest phenomenologically more accurate, meaning to the category "openness to the future" than does the temporal dialectic.

2. The second major principle of Niebuhr's interpretation of history is that the ontological structure of man, his "essential nature," remains constant throughout history as the precondition for history as history.[21]

[17] *ND*, 1:181–82.
[18] *ND*, 1:182–86.
[19] Ibid.
[20] *ND*, 1:271, 289.
[21] *ND*, 1:26, 170; 2:1–4, 256 ff.

The appearance of the historical future thus cannot in any way eradicate or eliminate this structure. As far as human nature is concerned, history is a continuum characterized by the same ontological structure. This structure, as we have noted, is expressed in many ways by Niebuhr: man is both creature and *imago dei*, finite and self-transcendent, bound by natural necessity and yet free, nature and spirit, vitality and form, individual and communal, partial and fragmentary and yet open to indeterminate possibilities, etc. He is, and will always be, full of these varied polarities; his philosophical self-understanding and social existence reflect the tension between these polarities—and always will. And through both his reflection and his concrete social existence man searches for resolutions of these tensions.

This permanence of ontological structure has three implications vis-à-vis the future. (*a*) Man in history is incurably creative, and so history is dynamic, moving, creative, and even progressive. Man as man is, has been, and will be "open" to the future; he can break old forms, establish new ones, and in turn transform them—in indeterminate fashion. This spiritual freedom over both past and present—essential to history as history—combines with man's undoubted rational abilities, his impulse for survival and well-being, his communal instincts and needs, and his moral urges to ensure that there are "indeterminate possibilities" for higher levels of technical development, of rational and moral insight, of social, legal, and political organization, and even thereby of freedom, justice, and individual realization.[22] New cultural forms will arise; they may well incarnate morally better or "higher" structures of common life—and there are no discernible limits that can be set to these developments except that man cannot shed his ontological structure as creature and as self-transcendent. Man is a creative, open being, and so his history, which he fashions, is open and creative to its end. Here, as Niebuhr reiterated, the Renaissance (and the Enlightenment and the nineteenth century) was right against the Reformation, and this sense of infinite possibilities in the future must be embodied in any valid contemporary theology.[23]

b) The permanence of man's freedom over structure—over both theoretical and social structures—means that no "final" (in the sense of permanent rather than excellent) society is possible or conceivable in history. Even if one abstracts from future possibility the dismantling

[22] *ND*, 2:84–85, 155–56, 190–92, 206–7, 209, 245–46, 256, 284; *FH*, pp. 2, 126, 199, 232.
[23] *ND*, 2:155–56, 190.

45

factors of sin and injustice, freedom would remain; and thus no particular social order can be regarded as permanent or stable. There is too
much vitality in any community; spirit always transcends any set
form of social cohesion; and thus any society—even an "ideal" one—is
subject to change, to a dissolution or a transformation of its structures.[24]
Niebuhr would not understand what could be meant by an "ideal"
society as a stable culmination of history if such were at all politically,
economically, and socially concrete—and so "historical"—in terms of
roles, social interrelations, modes of production, etc. This, again sin
aside, was a point of disagreement with Marx, for whom the forms of
social cohesion were created by the "higher logic" of the material
dialectic and not by human creativity, and thus, having themselves
molded human freedom, could never be threatened by it. Marx, said
Niebuhr, did not appreciate the spiritual creativity of man as a part
of his essential nature.[25] (c) If the ontological structure of man is
permanent in history, then the possibility of the "fall"—unless man
is substantially altered—remains while history lasts, since both that
possibility and the actuality of sin are derivative, though the latter
not by necessity, from man's ontological structure.[26] Again a stable,
redeemed society seems inconceivable if history remains history. This
leads to the next point.

3. As for Niebuhr the ontological structure of man remains constant
throughout history, characterizing the future as it has the past and the
present, so the ambiguous, "sinful" character of man's actualization
of that structure is a permanent characteristic of history.[27] The
possibility of the fall, which *possibility* is necessary as a part of our
ontological structure, becomes an inevitable *actuality*, though the latter
is not necessary. Sin for Niebuhr does not, therefore, arise from anything

[24] *ND*, 1:26–27, 38.
[25] *ND*, 1:45.
[26] See esp. *ND*, 1:251.
[27] *ND*, 2:36, 43, 54, 95–96, 155–56, 167, 208–9, 245–47, 251, 256; *FH*, pp. 15, 94, 123, 198, 232. It is not totally irrelevant vis-à-vis the general assessment of Niebuhr as "pessimistic" that the number of affirmations of the "indeterminate possibilities" of history (n. 22 above) are almost as many as those of its permanent ambiguity; in fact, in most cases the two affirmations stand side by side in the text. Of course these assertions that "on every level" history will remain ambiguous and so every future will share this ambiguity were made against developmental humanism. Still, as affirmations about the character of history, they would stand also in relation to an eschatological perfectionism for which the future is equally the locus of ultimate fulfillment, except for the difference that here it is the activity from the future of the transcendent God of the future rather than the immanent and developmental activity from past through present to future of immanent reason or deity.

essentially connected with temporal development, with the movement of time or the changes of history themselves, for example, a particular social structure, the influence of our animal past, or the influence of the cultural past.[28] Rather, sin arises out of the juxtaposition in man of finitude and freedom, out of his constant ontological structure—though not necessarily. Thus the possibility and the actuality of sin, the one necessary and the other inevitable, are stable in history, undeflected and certainly not eradicated by the movement of time. "Where there is history at all, there is freedom, where there is freedom, there is sin."[29] The vertical, not the temporal, dialectic is fully determinative here.

The permanent ambiguity of history is therefore as central a theme for Niebuhr as is that of the indeterminate possibilities of history—both characteristics flowing from man the prime maker of history. As the possibilities in history develop, as cultures rise higher, the possibilities for the sinful misuse of these developments rise too.[30] The problem of sin, of the religious rebellion of man against God and so of his immoral domination of his neighbor and his injustice to him, remains throughout history's course, not as a necessity but as an inevitability—and, for Niebuhr, as an indubitable deliverance of all historical experience. As long as man remains man, finite and self-transcendent, he will be tempted by anxiety about the impinging future; as long as he lacks perfect trust in and love of God, he will fall. For Niebuhr only if one adopted the most perfectionist sanctificationist position vis-à-vis the human future, where perfect faith becomes a stable human possession, could one conceive of future history as *not* characterized by this pattern of temptation and fall. And when one looks at the history of such sanctificationist hopes, even among those blessed by Christian wisdom and grace, it is clear that the problem of sin remains for them too.[31]

In arguing this point, which he did repeatedly, Niebuhr faced primarily humanistic groups who counted on man's developing reason, enshrined in cumulative techniques and progressing institutions, to eradicate man's inhumanity to man; and he faced secondarily historical Christian sanctificationist groups who felt that grace, once received in humility and faith, would transmute past sinfulness into perfection. He never faced an eschatological optimism about perfection

28 *ND*, 1:96 ff. Rather, as Niebuhr makes very clear, sin arises out of the ontological situation of man—though not with necessity—and so its possibility is a part of *all* history equally. See *ND*, 1:251.

29 *ND*, 2:80.

30 See esp. *ND*, 2:155–56, 245–46, 256; *FH*, pp. 94, 123, 232–33.

31 See esp. *ND* 2:120–26, 128–29. See also *ND*, 2:134–48, 169–80; *FH*, chap. 12.

in the future based neither on man's developing reason nor on grace working on human freedom, but on God's future action alone—a view in which it is not yet quite clear (at least to me) whether it is the future eradication of evil social structure (on the model of modern humanistic hopes), a new and totally effective dispensation of grace (on the model of sanctificationist groups), or simply "God's eschatological action from the future" which will clear sin at last away. In each case Niebuhr would, I believe, have pointed to the facts of past and present history and the deliverances of personal experience; and in both, to the evident dangers of pride or despair involved in the claims to share in such an ultimate redemptive action; and he would reassert his paradox of grace:[32] the more aware even the saints are of the continuation of their own sin—yes, especially when it has to do with their *future* actions[33]— the more hope there is that new possibilities of love will result. Grace is effective, and sin, he argued, is reduced—and will be reduced in any historical future—only insofar as awareness of the continuing presence of sin is there, repentence for that presence is felt, and thus openness to the other's possibilities is acknowledged. The Kingdom can become present only insofar as it is viewed as continually transcendent. And this, like the ontological structure of man, is the permanent character of history.[34]

One might add at this point another element from Niebuhr's political philosophy that is relevant to the question of the possibility in history of a perfect society of justice and love. For Niebuhr there is, granted the continuation of sin, an ineradicable tension between the possibilities of communal justice and the requirements of perfect love.[35] No matter how "just" a social structure may become—and there are, as I noted, indeterminate possibilities here—it can only approximate, it can never be or achieve, a community of love. Since any social scheme of justice in any history we know anything about presupposes self-concern and so the claims and counter-claims of each person or group, the community must be formed according to general rules, a universal system of law, and so be in some measure unfair to individual needs;

[32] *ND*, 2:124–25, 200–201, 213, 243.

[33] *ND*, 1:199–200, 258–59, 263; 2:137, 144; *FH*, pp. 201, 205, 229. For Niebuhr the "Pharisaic fallacy" is precisely the illusion that because I have known the sins in my own past, therefore I am promised the grace to be free of sins in the future. For him this assumption of a perfect future through grace is the epitome of self-righteousness.

[34] E.g., *ND*, 1:280; 2:95–96; *FH*, pp. 197–98.

[35] *ND*, 2:256–84; *FH*, pp. 189–200.

the order of the community must be enforced by a governmental power capable of whatever effective coercion is required and so a power whose potential misuse remains a possibility in all historical life; and at best the community can equalize but never eradicate the special interests and groups abounding in any historical community. So necessarily a potential instability of balance of power remains. Thus any historical society, however advanced in its structure, is prone to the possibility of the government appropriating to itself too much power (tyranny), the domination over the community of some special interest (aristocracy and oligarchy), or the unresolved conflict of groups in the wider community (anarchy).[36] The power of the sinful self to use and so to misuse structures of communal justice for its own purposes remains in history, whatever its legal and political level. Sin as well as spiritual freedom threatens the stability and benevolence of any social order: advances in social structure, like those in techniques and in knowledge, bring new possibilities of evil as well as of good. Sin arises finally from sinful men, not from anachronistic or unjust social structures. Thus, unless sin is assumed by some unexplained principle to be eradicated by the passage of time, no social structure in history, however highly developed, can expect to reflect the solution to history's deepest dilemma. A Kingdom of love continues to be relevant as a judgment and a lure to every historical approximation in terms of justice, but no historical order will perfectly incarnate such a society of love.[37] And the more it claims to do so, or to represent the road to it, the more the special interests and the governmental power that it actually represents and favors will feel justified in their domination of the other vitalities in the community.

There is here, let us note, a kind of watershed in theological argument. In conflict here are two quite different viewpoints about the meaning of the Gospel, an encounter that is hardly subject to empirical verification, since it has to do with the character of the yet *un*experienced future. Niebuhr appeals to the evidence of past experience with regard both to man as man in history and to man as inspired by grace. In both cases he points to the continuation of sin and so to the continuing relevance of the paradox of grace. If one assumes with him that history is a continuum in which both the ontological structure of man and the problem of sin remain, then these "empirical" arguments from past and present are surely overwhelming. The eschatologists, on the contrary, argue

[36] Esp. *ND*, 2:258, 284.
[37] E.g., *ND*, 2:49, 180; *FH*, pp. 193–94, 206, 233.

that the point of the Gospel is precisely the promise that the future will be different from the past and therefore that past experience "of the continuation of sin in the life of the redeemed" is irrelevant to the hope for God's new future when sin will *not* continue as it has in the past. Clearly the fundamental argument concerns what the promise of the Gospel is, and so what the relevance of evidence from past experience is: whether it is that God promises a new kind of future for history, or whether it is that God will in his own way make meaningful a history in which the human problem as evidenced in past and present experience remains to the end.[38]

Certainly one problem for the eschatologists in this debate is to delineate with some more precision how they understand "God's acts in the future" to be related to man's continuing freedom in future history, especially in *general* social and political history where not even a minimal Christian grace and sanctification can be assumed. For seemingly if the Kingdom is to be achieved in history, history being "open" and so effected in part by man's free decisions, unavoidably that achievement will be one in which human freedom participates— and so far that freedom *has* been "wayward." Or do they mean that the realization of the future Kingdom is to be effected solely by God's power, as eschatological symbols and most of their own language clearly imply? Is it in that case then a part of history, or in any meaningful sense history's culmination, since history as these men understand it is in large part the creative work of man's freedom? Or, as another alternative, does God for them really determine all of history from the future so that history is in that sense totally "eschatological" from beginning to end (eschatology implying action by God's power alone)? But then why is a God who "determines all from the future" in this manner not as responsible as any omnipotent God of Calvinism for the woes men now suffer from, for past and present tragedy as well as for future beatitude? These are questions which, it seems to me, eschatological theology must answer if, in the name of its interpretation of the Gospel, it is to deny—as it is surely free to do—Niebuhr's insistence that the evidence of past experience *is* relevant and thus that the Gospel addresses itself to a history in which sin continues, and promises a meaning to such a history.

[38] For the sharpness of the *theological* disagreement here, e.g., about what the Gospel in fact promises, see the following (which, incidentally, contains all the "axioms" so far explicated): "Thus the Christian faith does not promise to overcome the fragmentary and contradictory aspects of man's historic existence" (*FH*, p. 135).

4. In any case a basic axiom of Niebuhr's theology of history is that the future in historical time is a part of history as history has manifested itself in past and present experience, and not a qualitatively new aeon with regard either to the ontological structure of man, the problem of sin, or the relation of God's power to human freedom. If the Gospel, then, resolves the problem of history, as well as discloses its meaning— and Niebuhr agrees on the importance of that distinction [39]—it must resolve it on these terms, in the midst of the continuation (a) of human freedom, (b) of human sin, and (c) of the divine self-limitation vis-à-vis creaturely freedom. It was for this reason that Niebuhr explicitly rejected the traditional messianic and apocalyptic hope for history as the final victory of the righteous over the unrighteous, the consequent creation of a perfect society of the righteous, and so the manifestation in objective history of the divine power and rule.[40] Set in messianic and apocalyptic imagery, this traditional apocalyptic hope represents a literalistic form of the hope for history now "modernized" by the contemporary eschatologists. For them too the divine promise is for a qualitatively new social future, a realized society of perfect justice and love where history's oppressors will finally be overcome, the oppressed vindicated and raised to eminence and power, and so God's sovereignty and rule over history made manifest—that is, the divine power will reveal itself as actual or realized sovereignty. The divine judgment on sin is here transcended and resolved by the divine power as effective sovereignty over evil men and their evil works, not by the divine love as mercy toward evil men and their works. Niebuhr rejected this messianic answer to the problems of history of power and rule[41]— and so in principle the eschatologists' hope—because of the axioms we have outlined. If *all* are unrighteous, and will continue to be so in history, then a "final victory of the good over the evil," the ascent to power of the oppressed, obscures and possibly might increase the basic problem of history. For the "good" are also sinners, and certainly will be tempted to be more so if they claim and wield a totally righteous power. Oppressed are no more inherently virtuous than oppressors; their accession to power—as the accession of the previously down-trodden bourgeoisie shows—thus offers no relaxation to the dilemma of history; as Karl Popper has said: "Whatever class they [the rulers]

[39] *ND*, 2:47–52.
[40] *ND*, 2:19–34; *FH*, pp. 26–28.
[41] "God's sovereignty over history is established and his triumph over evil is effected not by the destruction of the evil-doers but by his own bearing of the evil" (*ND*, 2:46).

may have belonged to, once they are rulers, they belong to the ruling class." [42]

Since, moreover, it is the sin common to oppressors and oppressed, not the latter's state of oppression in a given social structure, that is the basic problem of history, it is a problem that will reappear in any social structure. Thus an improvement in social structure, however great and potentially creative, can at best relieve, mitigate, or decrease the moral problem of history, the domination of man by man; it cannot eradicate it once and for all. The meaning of history is not found, then, in the historical triumph of righteousness or the final achievement of a righteous society in history, because there are none who *are* absolutely righteous, and no fully righteous society is therefore a historical possibility. If God's only answer is to overcome the unrighteous, if the divine "triumph" in history is the triumph of righteous power against evil men and their works, then God must in the end destroy history itself in a judgment directed against everyone. [43] And through seeing in this way the ultimate issue of the messianic and apocalyptic hope to be a universal condemnation rather than the righteous victory the eschatologists had counted on—and, speaking historically, also the potential nemesis of self-destruction by a self-righteous society—Niebuhr was driven to understand the Christian meaning of history in quite different terms, in terms of reconciliation and the hope of historical renewal rather than the promise of total historical fulfillment.

5. The resolution of history's problems, then, is not in terms of the manifestation of divine power *over* evil but in terms of the manifestation of the divine love and mercy *to* evil—since all are unrighteous. The role of Christ is thus not to reveal the promise of a future divine sovereignty in history but to reveal in his life and death the divine mercy in, through, and beyond the divine judgment, to manifest the divine conquest of evil through forgiveness and renewal rather than through power and sovereignty, that is, in and through human freedom and not over it. Atonement rather than the Resurrection represents the center of the Gospel and is for Niebuhr—as the Resurrection with its promise of a new, qualitatively different future is for the eschatologists— the key to the interpretation of history. For in the Atonement the divine love in the person of Jesus takes history's evil onto itself through

[42] Karl R. Popper, "Prediction and Prophecy in the Social Sciences," in *Theories of History*, ed. P. Gardiner (Glencoe, Ill.: Free Press, 1959), p. 284.

[43] *ND*, 2:27.

suffering and thus makes possible a new relation of God to sinful men, and so a new life, "renewal," for sinful men.[44]

The divine will (precisely because it is righteous) cannot in Niebuhr's view reveal itself as sheer power, even as righteous power, and remain divine—unless, of course, it annihilates human freedom and so history. For all power in history, even that which seems most righteous, is, as we have seen, necessarily partial and in actuality corrupted. This means that in history (assuming the continuity of history's character) the divine righteousness and love must reveal themselves precisely as powerlessness, for only this—and not the victory of the good—represents the perfection of *agape*. And powerlessness in a sinful history means suffering.[45] The final revelation of divine sovereignty in history, and so the meaning of history, is a revelation of powerlessness and of suffering at the hands of evil rather than victory over evil—that is, a revelation of judgment and forgiveness and renewal of evil rather than the crushing or removal of it. No greater distinction from the messianic hope of a divine rule over evil can be imagined.[46] As Niebuhr once put this difference: "Thus the suffering of the guiltless, which is the primary problem of life for those who look at it from the standpoint of their own virtues, is made into the ultimate answer of history for those who look at it from the standpoint of the problematic character of all human virtue."[47]

The suffering of divine love on the Cross is not only the sole possibility of the *divine* resolution of an ambiguous history's meaning; it is also the only way that a resolution of that problem can be effective in and through men who retain their freedom and continually reenact the problem of sin. For judgment on their sin as well as mercy toward it is mediated in the Cross, and thus are repentance and humility as well as new trust in God possible for men. Repentance at the continuing reality of their own sin and trust in the divine will for themselves and for the history in which they live are the inward, human bases for "renewal" in life, a new attitude of humility toward our own works—and social structures—and a new confidence in the future necessary to mitigate the inevitable anxiety about that future.[48] The Atonement,

[44] *ND*, 2:35, 54–57, 67, 211–12; 1:142–43, 147–48; *FH*, pp. 141–50.

[45] *ND*, 2:42–47.

[46] See esp. *ND*, 2:45.

[47] *ND*, 2:45; *FH*, p. 142.

[48] For the relation of atonement, justification, and grace to man's inward appropriation and response in terms of repentance, humility, trust, and a new life of self-forgetfulness, love, etc.—i.e., to "renewal"—see esp. *ND*, 2:100–126.

then, is the only principle for historical renewal on the basis of which the creativity of man can form a new future without demonic destruction.

For Niebuhr, then, meaning in history is not achieved by a final manifestation of the divine power. Rather, it is defined by two intra-historical modes of divine activity which therefore are paradoxical in form: on the one hand, by the manifestation of the divine atoning love in *powerlessness* leading to the possibility of the renewal of freedom; and on the other, by the *hidden* work of providence in history. Love is powerless in history because it works on and through human freedom; providence is hidden because it also does its work in and through freedom. It works by judging each reappearance of evil, by bringing harmony out of what was not intended by men as harmonious, and by luring or "beguiling" men into new possibilities of good—and thus transmuting the creative achievements of men, designed mainly for their own well-being, into creative rather than destructive channels.[49] History does have provisional achievements of meaning. Through the intermingling of providence and freedom there are indeterminate possibilities of higher levels of development; because of God's providential judgment there are limits to the destructive use of these levels; and because of the divine judgment and mercy in Christ there are continual possibilities of renewal.

These divine activities in history, namely, the work of providence and of atoning love, must, however, be appropriated by and so move through human freedom to be creatively effective.[50] History for Niebuhr, much more than for the eschatologists (for whom God "masters the present from the future" and apparently will do so

[49] Niebuhr never wrote a systematic discussion of providence. Often he referred to it (or seemed to do so) as "grace" or "common grace." For examples of the usage referred to in the text, see *ND*, 1:277; *FH*, pp. 27–28, 36–37, 175, 222. For a most interesting and helpful discussion of "grace" as providence in Niebuhr's thought, see J. Keith Keeling, "The Transcendence of Grace in the Theology of Reinhold Niebuhr" (Ph.D. diss., University of Chicago, 1974).

[50] The relation of atonement (and the same is true of providence) to human freedom or autonomy is clear in the following: "It [the Atonement] alone was seen to have the power to overcome the recalcitrance of man *at the very center of man's personality*, however successful the divine power might be to set outer limits beyond which human defiance could not go" (*FH*, pp. 142–43; emphasis added). The same interrelation of divine activity and freedom is the theological basis for the "existential" element that permeates Niebuhr's thought. Niebuhr is clear throughout that only if the work of God—in revelatory grace or in providence—is existentially or inwardly appropriated, is it truly effective in renewal. Both providence and grace in history must work *through* free and autonomous appropriation by man if they are to "work." For this existential element in Niebuhr, see esp. *ND*, 1:205 ff., 257–60; 2:47, 56–57, 61, 100–126, 231; *FH*, pp. 101, 126, 140, 142, 151.

completely at the end), is primarily the work of human freedom in both its creative and its destructive aspects. Thus is it ambiguous throughout its course. God works in and on the human freedom that creates history, and thus is there meaning in history. But God works in and through human freedom, and so, that freedom being fallible and fallen, fulfillment is never complete. If, in contrast to the eschatologists, Niebuhr is a "pessimist" about history, it is therefore because he is an "Arminian" and not an absolutist even about the future. For him the judgment involved in the self-destruction of pride or the law of revelation must be known and appropriated inwardly by *freedom* in repentance, if it is to lead to renewal and so to avoid nemesis and despair; new possibilities beyond the old order must be envisioned freely by men in order to become incarnate in history; men must be beguiled by common grace in order to transcend their own interests; trust in providence must become an actual character of our autonomy if it is to lead to a new future; self-sacrificial love must qualify mutual love if communities are to be really creative. In other words, renewal, though never complete, is for Niebuhr the principle of hope in history rather than eschatological fulfillment because such partial renewal is a possibility of human freedom under providence and grace, whereas total fulfillment is not. If history is to continue to be *history*, providence and the divine mercy must even in the future continue to work in conjunction with freedom. Thus the assumption of the permanence of the divine self-limitation in relation to freedom is the third important axiom in this view of history. Through its work on freedom divine grace deflects the creativity of spirit away from destructive paths and grants it the continual possibility of creative renewal. But by the same token, because grace thus works through freedom, fulfillment is never complete, and every partial achievement continues until the end to stand under the judgment of God and the lure of the still transcendent Kingdom.

6. Although for Niebuhr all of history stands under the divine judgment until its end, and at no level of achievement can any concrete social order appear as "righteous" before God or perfectly reveal the rule and so the being of God, still for him all civilizations, social orders, and groups in history are by no means equal in virtue or in worth.[51] Some are morally more creative than others and thus must be either defended if they already exist (as in the defense of democracy against fascism or, say, that of Allende against the United States) or brought

[51] *ND*, 1:214, 223–27.

into being if they are "not-yet" possibilities. Correspondingly, relatively unjust orders must be criticized intellectually and refashioned politically from the inside, or resisted if they attack from the outside. And in all cases force may be required: in defense of a better order, in the reform of a potentially improvable order (as in the case of the struggle for unions), or finally in revolution against a hopelessly unjust and recalcitrant order. These relative judgments between social orders, based on relative distinctions between healthy and unhealthy social possibilities, are the stuff of politics—and that after all was what theological symbols, including that of the Atonement, were for. Niebuhr was always more disgusted with an apolitical orthodoxy than with a utopian liberalism, and he argued more vehemently with a Barthian transcendence of political distinctions than with a progressivist identification of social reform with Christianity. Thus Niebuhr never conceived of subverting these relative political judgments through theology, since it was precisely as the creative framework for them that he conceived and reconceived his theology.[52] He held to a theology of atonement, justification, and reconciliation as opposed to a messianic theology of a divine victory over evil men and evil orders, because he felt the former was a better *political* theology than the latter—and, note, better in terms of its possibilities for achieving justice, freedom, and humanity in history. He was sure that only if confidence in one's social cause is well salted with a humble consciousness of the relativity and ambiguity of that cause, can that cause be saved from pride and so ultimate cruelty and self-destruction. His theology of atonement, justification, and the paradox of grace was not designed to eradicate hope for the future but precisely to eradicate the nemesis of self-destructive fanaticism and the despair that arise therefrom. His theology sought to provide the most creative ground of political action possible. Even at its seemingly most impractical and theological, it was always a political theology, the theoretical ground for *praxis*.

The theological basis for relative political and moral judgments in history was Niebuhr's familiar and oft-criticized distinction between the equality of sin (and so the need for atoning grace and justification for all) and the inequality of guilt (that men are *not* equal in the injustice, oppression, and so suffering they cause for others).[53] Whether

[52] His two central courses at Union Seminary from 1947 through 1949 were "History of Christian Ethics" (and that meant social ethics largely) and "A Theological Framework for Social Ethics."
[53] Ibid.

this is or is not a helpful usage of the word "guilt," the distinction Niebuhr intends here is crucial. If one forgets the equality of sin in the oppressed as well as the oppressors and in the good as well as the bad (as humanistic, sanctificationist, and eschatological perfectionisms are apt to do), then pride, fanaticism, and cruelty of either a conservative or a radical sort are bound to result;[54] if one forgets the inequality of guilt (as mysticism, monasticism, Lutheranism, withdrawing sects, and pacifists are apt to do), then no creative participation in politics or civilization is possible. Niebuhr was clear that the principle underlying the inequality of guilt is the factor of *power*.[55] Whenever an ego has gained power, then its sin has worse consequences on others than when that ego has no power. The wealthy, the politically powerful, the distinguished, the wise, the good—they are not more sinful than ordinary people, though they may in many ways be more tempted; rather, their power makes their sin more effective and so more destructive. Thus Niebuhr combines the clear biblical "prejudice" against the mighty with the biblical message of the unrighteousness of all into a quite new synthesis: a revolutionary theology against the mighty of the earth as primarily "guilty," with a theology of atonement, justification, and the transcendence of the Kingdom because of the equality of sin.

We should note the important implications for the future possibilities of history latent in this oft-ridiculed doctrine. If inequality of guilt (consequences that entail suffering) arises from inequality of power, then clearly "indeterminate advances" in the economic, political, and social spheres, higher levels of legal and social justice—which Niebuhr recognized as possible if not probable in the future—can, if they reduce imbalances of power in economic, political, and social life, reduce suffering as well. Even if sin remains, the amount of "guilt" can in principle be reduced in the future if unjust distribution and so inequality of power are reduced. Niebuhr clearly recognized vast differences in distribution of power, in guilt, and so in suffering between contemporary societies—otherwise political judgments would be irrelevant. The same distinction makes just as much sense between successive social orders in the course of history and so provides a basis in his thought for hope for the future. Again no such society can be

[54] See *ND*, 1:199–200, 226 (the danger of moral pride as especially the problem of the "good and of the oppressed") and 1:227 (the necessity of the symbol of the universality and so equality of sin to puncture the pretensions of the "good" who are successful).

[55] *ND*, 1:222–26.

either permanent or perfect, *the* Kingdom. But that suffering can be reduced is surely the presupposition of all political action, and Niebuhr both recognized that and gave it a new base in his political theology.

7. It is clear from all we have said about Niebuhr's view of future history that eschatological symbols have a very different role in his theology than in that of the contemporary eschatologists. The vertical dialectic of transcendence, not the temporal dialectic of eschatology, defines his use of all theological symbols; and thus the vertical dialectic defines his use of eschatological symbols rather than the reverse. This means, as has been abundantly clear, that eschatology does not here function as defining the character of the historical future as opposed to the past, that is, as fulfillment as the locus in historical time of total and manifest divine sovereignty, as in effect the place where history and God's being merge and become one *in history*. Eschatology, on the contrary, is one of the ways—the way concerned with the future and so with *finis* and *telos*—that the vertical dialectic between transcendence and history is maintained. Thus eschatology means precisely the opposite here: not that the future in history is the locus of divine fulfillment, but that it is precisely *not* that locus, that all historical achievements are partial, that all of history stands under a transcendent judgment and points to a transcendent fulfillment, and so that the final meaning of history transcends history—and yet that history's achievements are not annulled but fulfilled beyond history.[56] Eschatology expresses the same principle of the permanence of ambiguity in history, the possibility of history's improvement, the Atonement and renewal, and the paradox of grace and a transcendent fulfillment which we have noted. Eschatology represents this dialectic from the point of view of the ultimate manifestation of that transcendence with which history in all its facets is always related, in other words, in terms of the ultimate divine sovereignty beyond history rather than of the divine involvement in history. Here the hidden power of God in history becomes the ultimate divine sovereignty beyond history; the permanent ambiguity of history becomes the Anti-Christ; the hidden and partial judgments of history become here an ultimate judgment; forgiveness, mercy, and acceptance through suffering *agape* become here the ultimate triumph of the divine love in the Parousia; and the relative creative renewals of history become the promise of the final Kingdom. Each one of these eschatological symbols points to the divine as

[56] See the summary of the meaning of eschatological symbols in *ND*, 2:50–52, as well as the fuller discussion in ibid., chap. 10.

transcendent to all of history's possibilities, as God always is; and yet as the ultimate representation of that transcendence whose impingement on history makes history possible, each *as transcendent* is related to and ingredient in each of history's moments. The Kingdom is a judgment and a lure for all historical social achievement; its essential role and meaning *in* history is precisely in that transcendence and would be lost the moment it was regarded as directly ingredient in history. Then it would become either impotent as incredible or demonic as believed. For Niebuhr, eschatology, like the Creation, sets the primary symbolic horizon within which history can be understood as it really is, as related to a transcendent reality which is ultimately sovereign but which can never be identified with history, a reality which is the horizon within which creative renewal in history in relation to that transcendence as love and as grace becomes possible, and a reality whose forgiving love accepts all of creative historical life into reunion with itself. Eschatology, therefore, stands definitely under the more central paradox of grace and so the vertical dialectic; it is a legitimate culmination of Niebuhr's theology but by no means its center.

*   *   *

Let us summarize our re-presentation of Niebuhr's theology of history in the light of futurist eschatology by employing in this new context some of the large typologies which dominated his own thinking about himself and others. As he said explicitly, he wished to make a synthesis of Renaissance and Reformation emphases in understanding history, that is, to combine the Renaissance emphasis (and actually that of the eighteenth and nineteenth centuries as well) on *growth* and *development* in history ("indeterminate possibilities of advance") with the Reformation emphasis on the continuation of sin in the life of the redeemed and so the continual need for divine grace and justification.[57] Thus, again explicitly, he made the innovative move of interpreting *history* in terms of the symbols—heretofore used in relation to *individual* existence—of atonement, justification, and renewal.[58] We have seen how this theme of justification and renewal intertwines with that of creativity and of indeterminate possibilities and yet remains dominant over it. Since (1) moral renewal as the outgrowth of justification is so powerful a theme in Niebuhr, since (2) the importance of moral discrimination and judgment between relative social values and also

[57] See esp. *ND*, 2:204–12.
[58] See *ND*, 2:35, 55, 67; *FH*, p. 139; *ND*, 1:142–43, 146–48.

of moral political action is evident in his thought, and yet (3) the theme of justification remains the dominant motif, one can say that the synthesis he achieved was one which combined a Calvinistic (rather than a Lutheran) form of the Reformation with the modern sense of unlimited possibility—which should surprise no one familiar with Niebuhr's overwhelmingly moral and political interpretation of existence. As with Calvin, justification in Niebuhr is teleological, leading to a more fruitful moral and political existence, and so in relation to history to a more creative and human social order in the future. Because it was in a humanistic, moralistic, and optimistic culture that Niebuhr emphasized sin and justification, he was mistaken as "merely a Lutheran" who separated law and Gospel so far as to be unable to bring them together again. No interpretation of Niebuhr could be further from the truth, I think; all of the Calvinistic moral passion and implicit moral and political teleology in time was in him. However, this "Calvinism" was now set within the new atmosphere created by the Enlightenment and the nineteenth century of (1) a moving historical temporality inclusive of *all* history; (2) a sense of the inalienable *autonomy* and *self-creativity* of human freedom; (3) a sense of the relevance of secular *social* structures and institutions to sin, grace, and redemption; (4) a wide world of *relative* viewpoints and so of tolerance; and (5) an *existential* and *pragmatic* rather than legalistic view of truth and of morals. Thus did what he calls the Renaissance have far more of an effect on his "Calvinism" then merely to inject indeterminate possibilities into his view of history! And let us recall that it was only to optimistic humanists and fervent apocalyptists that Calvinism was regarded as "pessimistic" with regard to the moral possibilities of life and of historical communities.

In terms of Niebuhr's typology, the eschatologists also reflect the Renaissance: (1) in their emphasis on the development of world and secular history as the prime locus of the divine promises; (2) in their emphasis on an open history and on freedom (however provisional); (3) in their insistence that the redemption of secular social structures is the purpose of God's eschatological action; (4) in their "temporalistic" reinterpretation of eschatology as qualifying and determining the moving process of ordinary historical time "from the moving future" rather than merely qualifying its last moments; and (5) above all in their faith that the temporal and historical *future* is the locus and even the principle of ultimate redemption. In all of this, despite their apocalyptic language and their strange, reversed causality, their theologies express major themes of the Renaissance and of modernity. Which of these, Niebuhr or the eschatologists, is more influenced by modernity is hard to say since both are overwhelmingly so. My own opinion is that points 4 and 5 above are so central in their theology and so clearly the work of modernity, that, strangely, contemporary eschatology is more the product of that modern developmental view of time it tends to deplore than is Niebuhr's thought, whose central principle of transcendence is by no means drawn from any aspect of modernity.

As their arguments with Ernst Bloch show, however, the eschatologists are not merely "modernist." The divine functions centrally here in their eschatology, though, as noted, it was not clear *how* it functioned. Since for them eschatology provides the principles for the interpretation of the ordinary passage of time, of the whole process of history, rather than merely its end (points 3 and 4 above), the eschatological action of God cannot be thought of in purely literal apocalyptic terms—as they are wont to speak of it—that is, as action by God alone and not also by man. If an "apocalyptic" interpretation of *that* sort is made of their eschatology, as noted, history is divested of human freedom and events are simply what "God ordains from the future," a position they all abhor and vigorously reject (although in its older Calvinist form). Thus for them in some sense God must work from the future through human freedom in his eschatological action in general history. That is, some mode of "sanctification" through divine grace, now clearly wider than "Christian" grace in the covenant community, must be at work in general history. And equally clearly, because there is a real contrast with Niebuhr on history's possibilities, and so in the effects of grace, this is a *perfectionist* theory of sanctification, since as a result of the divine work the future becomes qualitatively different and perfection is achieved. As with Wesley, the point of the Gospel for the eschatologists is that in history the fulness of perfection is not only promised but achieved—God's glory will manifest itself unequivocally in and through the creature. Since, therefore, they have "demythologized" apocalyptic language about the end into a form of speech interpreting the continuing passage of historical time, into language about historical process, the eschatologists represent, it seems to me, a synthesis of Renaissance with Wesleyan perfectionism, not of apocalyptic and Marxism as they maintain. And thus (as anyone familiar with Niebuhr's view of Wesley will remember!) does their viewpoint contrast so vividly at every point with his. That the Wesleyan confidence in the possibilities of future perfection has been creative theologically, morally, and politically there can be little doubt. But whether such a synthesis is the best vehicle for interpreting man's social and political hopes and the possibilities of his future in grace is, to me at least, a matter of some debate and one to which what Niebuhr has to say has a continuing relevance.

Reinhold Niebuhr's Theistic Ethic

Franklin I. Gamwell

I

Whatever disputes have characterized recent theological discussion, it seems fair to say that two propositions are now widely affirmed in theological circles: (1) A contemporary theological formulation should include an explicit response to the challenge of secularism. (2) A contemporary theological formulation should include a positive interpretation of political life. It might be further suggested that these imperatives are tantamount to the demand that theology be, as some have put it, secular but not secularistic—that is, theological understanding should provide an unqualified affirmation of human concern for this world and its affairs while insisting that the worth of this world depends upon some transcendent reality.[1] Whatever the merit of this further suggestion, however, the same two imperatives provide a context within which the importance of Reinhold Niebuhr's achievement can be appreciated. For Niebuhr's intellectual enterprise, in large measure at least, may be understood as an attempt to purge twentieth-century political affirmations of secularistic convictions.

This description of Niebuhr's thought is repeated in saying that he attempts to formulate an alternative to those he came to call the "foolish children of light" and the "cynical children of darkness."[2] To put the matter in this way is again to identify political thought as a principal telos of Niebuhr's work—for these "children" are adherents of fundamentally different political positions. It is less obvious but also true that Niebuhr's response to secularism is implied here. Since Niebuhr holds that human existence is "incurably religious," in the sense that one cannot act without some "overt or covert presupposition"

[1] A clear presentation of the distinction between secular and secularistic is found in Shubert M. Ogden, *The Reality of God* (New York: Harper & Row, 1966), pp. 1–13.

[2] See Reinhold Niebuhr, *The Children of Light and the Children of Darkness* (New York: Charles Scribner's Sons, 1944 [new foreword, 1960]), esp. chap. 1. All references are to Niebuhr's works unless otherwise specified.

regarding "the totality of things conceived as a realm of meaning," [3] both types of "children" are secularistic, in the sense that they presume the "center and source of . . . meaning" [4] to be within the world. The "foolish children of light" are not secularistic by virtue of being "children of light" (i.e., because they "seek to bring self-interest under the discipline of a more universal law and in harmony with a more universal good"), [5] but rather because they are "foolish"—that is, because they presume that the "center and source" of this universal good is, or at least will be, within history. They have "a touching faith in the possibility [not to say inevitability] of achieving a simple harmony between self-interest and the general welfare." [6] The "children of darkness," on the other hand, "know no law beyond their own will and interest" [7]—or, at best, the will and interest of a particular community. If they are cynical because they affirm no universal law, they are also secularistic because the denial of universal law implies a particular source of meaning, and such is, by definition, within the world. Moreover, "foolish" universalism and particularism exhaust the possibilities open to political theory within secularistic convictions. Consequently, the attempt to provide an alternative to these types is perforce the attempt to formulate political theory within theistic convictions, that is, consistent with the claim that the center and source of meaning is beyond the self and the world [8] or transcendent to history.

For Niebuhr, however, theistic religious convictions are not always consistent with a concern for politics and political theory. On the contrary, the transcendent source of meaning is sometimes understood to be exclusive of history. "Classical idealism and mysticism" deny the meaning of politics in particular and history in general in the name of some rational or nonrational eternity which "swallows up all particularity." [9] Niebuhr therefore distinguishes such theistic denials of history, which we may call those of "classicism," from his own position, which we may call "authentic theism." Authentic theism, then, affirms a source of meaning which is not only transcendent to but also inclusive of history—and, consequently, affirms the meaning of

[3] "Religion and Action," in *Science and Man*, ed. Ruth Nada Anshen (New York: Harcourt Brace & Co., 1942), p. 44; see also *The Nature and Destiny of Man*, 2 vols. (New York: Charles Scribner's Sons, 1941–43), 1:13–14.

[4] "Religion and Action," p. 45.

[5] *Children of Light*, p. 101.

[6] Ibid., p. 7.

[7] Ibid., p. 9.

[8] See, e.g., *Nature and Destiny*, 1:14.

[9] Ibid., 2:11, 13.

politics. Since, for Niebuhr, the religious alternatives are exhausted by secularism and theism, his own religious conviction may be defined negatively as being neither secularistic nor classical: "Without the presuppositions of the Christian faith [equivalent, for Niebuhr, to authentic theism], men run into the Charybdis of life-denial and acosmism [classicism] in the effort to escape the Scylla of idolatry [secularism]. Either they make some contingent and relative vitality or coherence into the unconditioned principle of meaning or they negate the whole of temporal and historical existence because it is involved in contingency." [10]

This essay will not attempt direct consideration of either Niebuhr's understanding of divinity or his political theory. Rather, its purpose is to examine Niebuhr's thought at a point through which his theism and political theory are systematically related—that is, to examine his theistic ethic. [11] It may well be true, as some have suggested, that

---

[10] Ibid., 1:166. Niebuhr's typology of religious convictions may be summarized schematically as shown in the table below.

Source of Meaning Is			
Transcendent to History		Not Transcendent to History	
THEISM		SECULARISM	
Transcendent Source of Meaning Is		Historical Source of Meaning Is	
Inclusive of History	Not Inclusive of History	Universal	Particular
AUTHENTIC or CHRISTIAN THEISM	CLASSICISM	"FOOLISH" UNIVERSALISM	PARTICUL-ARISM

Niebuhr's use of the term "religion" is not consistent throughout his writings. At the least, one may identify two different meanings. Narrowly used, the term indicates the affirmation that some reality beyond or transcendent to the world is the source of meaning—in which case "secularism" is used in contrast to "religion" (see, e.g., *Children of Light*, esp. chap. 1). Broadly used, "religion" indicates simply a conviction regarding the source of meaning—in which case "secularism" is a religious type. To repeat the point, "religion" (narrowly used) indicates the theistic type of "religion" (broadly used). This essay fastens upon the latter meaning of the term.

[11] The matter may be put with additional precision: For Niebuhr, every answer to the religious question (i.e., what is the source of meaning?) implies and is implied by some answer to the ethical question (i.e., what is the norm of human existence?). In terms somewhat foreign to Niebuhr, we may say that there is, for him, no fundamental separation between fact and value—and just this is intended in saying that

Niebuhr did not give sustained attention to formulating a doctrine of God.[12] But it is quite clear that a proper understanding of the ethic implied in Christian convictions, and the reasons for its superiority to alternatives, constituted one of his principal intellectual concerns. And his constructive political theory was, in large measure at least, an attempt to elucidate the "relevance" of that ethic to the problems of human communities. Consequently, it seems fair to say that an examination of Niebuhr's theism in relation to his interpretation of political life must include an analysis of his ethic—and it is that analysis which this essay undertakes. The next section of this paper will attempt to explicate that ethic and Niebuhr's argument for it; the concluding section will offer an assessment. In sum, the paper will attempt to argue that Niebuhr's position is internally inconsistent. His theistic ethic is, I will try to show, incoherent with the understanding of authentic theism presented above—and that because the ethic is, in Niebuhr's own terms, implicitly classical in character.

II

Since authentic theism understands the transcendent reality to be the center and source of "the totality of things conceived as a realm of meaning," Niebuhr frequently designates "the norm of human existence" with the term "harmony"—that is, a total or perfect harmony. "He [man] knows that he ought to act so as to assume his rightful place in the harmony of the whole."[13] Thus, the "original righteousness" of human existence is said to be "a harmony between the soul and God . . . , a harmony within the soul . . . , and a harmony between the self and neighbor."[14] Or, again: "It is not the highest perfection of man to achieve a unity of being from which all natural and historical vitalities have been subtracted. The highest unity is a harmony of love in which the self relates itself in its freedom to other selves in their freedom under the will of God."[15]

---

religious convictions concern the totality of things conceived as a realm of *meaning*. Moreover, because politics is included within the totality of things, every political theory, at least in some respects, implies and is implied by some answer to the ethical question.

[12] See, e.g., Ronald H. Stone, *Reinhold Niebuhr: Prophet to Politicians* (Nashville, Tenn.: Abingdon Press, 1972), pp. 225–26.

[13] *Beyond Tragedy* (New York: Charles Scribner's Sons, 1937), pp. 295–96; see also *Children of Light*, pp. 9, 73.

[14] *Nature and Destiny*, 1:286; see also pp. 288–89.

[15] Ibid., p. 95.

Because he holds Christian theism to be authentic, Niebuhr also believes that the character of divinity and the norm of human existence are disclosed through the special events constitutive of the Christian faith. And when Niebuhr's attention is focused here, he speaks of the norm as one of "sacrificial love." [16] The sacrificial life and death of Christ represents "the perfect disinterestedness of the divine love" and, simultaneously, the *agape* or sacrificial love which is "conformity to the will of God." [17] As the divine will to which it conforms, sacrificial love is "disinterested," a definition which is frequently replaced in Niebuhr's exposition by the terms "heedless" and "uncalculating." While there are times when these terms tend to suggest an activity which is "ecstatic" or "spontaneous" in a sense to which thinking is alien, [18] in the main Niebuhr understands this norm in contrast to all imperatives which affirm attention to one's own self-interest. *Agape* is "a love 'which seeketh not its own'"; "what is demanded is an action in which regard for the self is completely eliminated." [19] Sacrificial love is disinterested in, heedless to, or uncalculating of the consequences to self—which is to say that the Christian ethic is one of "pure nonresistance." [20] The "final goodness," to repeat the point again, "stands in contradiction to all forms of human goodness in which self-assertion and love are compounded." [21]

These two designations of the authentic norm complicate a reading of Niebuhr's ethic—for, at the least, it is not immediately apparent that "perfect harmony" and "sacrificial love" are equivalent. On the one hand, the meaning of "perfect harmony" would seem to include

[16] Ibid., 2:68.

[17] Ibid., pp. 72, 84.

[18] See, e.g., *Faith and History* (New York: Charles Scribner's Sons, 1949), p. 184.

[19] *Nature and Destiny*, 2:72; 1:287.

[20] *Christianity and Power Politics* (New York: Charles Scribner's Sons, 1940), pp. 9–10; see also *Nature and Destiny*, 2:72. Niebuhr's identification of *agape* with the ethic of nonresistance insofar disproves any presumption that he means by sacrificial love simply the willingness to sacrifice the self whenever such is required for the greatest good of all. In his polemic against pacifism, for instance, he is quite clear that self-assertion is *always* a compromise of the Christian ethic. "The pacifists . . . are forced to recognize that an ethic of pure non-resistance can have no immediate relevance to any political situation; for in every political situation it is necessary to achieve justice by resisting pride and power. They therefore declare that the ethic of Jesus is not an ethic of non-resistance, but one of non-violent resistance; that it allows one to resist evil provided the resistance does not involve the destruction of life or property. . . . There is not the slightest support in Scripture for this doctrine of non-violence. Nothing could be plainer than that the ethic uncompromisingly enjoins non-resistance and not non-violent resistance" (*Power Politics*, pp. 9–10).

[21] *Nature and Destiny*, 2:89.

some affirmation of the self—simply because the self is included within the totality. On the other hand, such an affirmation seems to be precisely what the term "sacrificial love" proscribes. At first blush, in other words, one might be led to ask whether Niebuhr in fact presents us with one or two theistic norms.[22] Whatever the merit of that question, however, it is important to recognize that no such question exists for Niebuhr himself. Indeed, nothing seems clearer in Niebuhr's ethical discussion than his intention to identify these two terms. Not only does he use both to define the norm of human existence, but his phrase "the law of love," which refers to the same norm, appears in some contexts as synonymous with "*agape*" and in others as synonymous with "perfect harmony."[23] Moreover, in more than one passage, he explicitly equates the two: "The "essential,' the normative man, is thus a 'God-man' whose sacrificial love seeks conformity with, and finds justification in, the divine and eternal *agape*, the ultimate and final harmony of life with life."[24] "The principle of equal affirmation of all life is closest to the ideal of sacrificial love, in which each life is subjected to the necessities of life as such. Yet equality is only an approximation of love. The ideal of love fulfills and transcends all law. It fulfills it in the sense that it completes what every high moral law implies. It transcends it in the sense that it presupposes a harmony of life with itself and all life which man in history never realizes."[25] And it is within an extended discussion of perfect harmony that Niebuhr writes: "What is demanded is an action in which regard for the self is completely eliminated."[26] The present section of this essay will attempt to clarify Niebuhr's ethic by

[22] To my knowledge, Daniel Day Williams was the first to point this out. If "'the highest unity is a harmony of love in which the self relates itself in its freedom to other selves in their freedom under the will of God,'" Williams argues, "where is the 'ultimate contradiction' between the self-assertion of the human life and the divine *agape?*" (*God's Grace and Man's Hope* [New York: Harper & Bros., 1949], pp. 75–76).

[23] For the former, see, e.g., *Nature and Destiny*, 2:92; *Faith and History*, pp. 173–79. For the latter, see, e.g., *Nature and Destiny*, 2:244; "Christian Faith and the Common Life," in *Christian Faith and Common Life*, Nils Ehrenström et al. (Chicago: Willett, Clark & Co., 1938), p. 71.

[24] *Nature and Destiny*, 2:81.

[25] "Common Life," p. 94. One might also note the following citation: "The real fact is that the absolute character of the ethic of Jesus conforms to the actual constitution of man and history, that is, to the transcendent freedom of man over the contingencies of nature and the necessities of time, so that only a final harmony of life with life in love can be the ultimate norm of his existence" (*Nature and Destiny*, 2:50–51).

[26] Ibid., 1:287.

showing why he thinks that these two formulations of the ultimate imperative are substantively identical.

The identity intended by Niebuhr is rephrased in saying that both sacrificial love and perfect harmony are, for him, neither classical nor secularistic. For both, then, refer to the authentic norm. Classical ethics assume a transcendent source of meaning exclusive of history and thus call for "escape from history" either through "contemplation of" and/or "final incorporation into" "an undifferentiated unity of life in eternity." [27] To the contrary, perfect harmony "is not a unity of being from which all natural and historical vitalities have been subtracted," and sacrificial love "is an act within history." [28] Secularistic ethics deny a transcendent source of meaning. To the contrary, sacrificial love "presupposes a harmony . . . which man in history never realizes." [29] As one might expect, it is principally through the contrast with secularistic ethics that Niebuhr develops his own—and that contrast, therefore, provides an approach to clarity regarding the normative identity of *agape* and perfect harmony in his thought.

More especially, Niebuhr's theistic ethic may be better understood in distinction from the ethic of "mutual love," which is the term he frequently uses for "the highest good" known "from the standpoint of history," [30] that is, within secularistic convictions. Obedience to this norm appears to be defined by the aim at reciprocity of advantages between the self and other or others. "Only in mutual love, in which the concern of one person for the interests of another prompts and elicits a reciprocal affection, are the social demands of historical existence satisfied." [31] One must not infer that Niebuhr intends here an activity in which the agent's concern for another is a means toward serving his own interest—an activity which, at best, is informed by "a prudent regard for the interests of the self." [32] It is true that a few of his statements make this inference plausible.[33] On the whole, however, Niebuhr is clear that prudential self-interest is a corruption of mutual love—and the two are easily confused, perhaps, because, as we shall presently discuss, Niebuhr holds that human activity inevitably degenerates into this corruption when mutual love is assumed to be the

[27] Ibid., 2:71, 90, 68.
[28] Ibid., pp. 95, 68.
[29] "Common Life," p. 94.
[30] *Nature and Destiny*, 2:68–69; see also pp. 81–82.
[31] Ibid., p. 69; see also p. 247.
[32] Ibid., p. 96.
[33] See, e.g., *Faith and History*, p. 176.

ultimate norm. Nonetheless, the norm prescribes an activity which aims at *mutual* advantages through reciprocity or cooperation. The self is simply one among the more than one whose interests are pursued. "Coherence and consistency in the whole realm of historical vitality" demand that "all claims within the general field of interests must be proportionately satisfied and related to each other harmoniously." [34] Mutual love, then, regards the interests of all relevant individuals to be in some sense equal in merit. "In mutual love and distributive justice the self regards itself as an equal but not as a specially privileged member of a group in which the rational self seeks to apportion the values of life justly or to achieve perfect reciprocity of advantages." [35]

Mutual love is *secularistic*, in Niebuhr's understanding, because activity which takes this as the ultimate imperative presumes to be "justified by historical consequences." [36] To the best of my reading, Niebuhr never indicates precisely what he means by the term "justification," but his intention in the present context may be plausibly inferred. Consider the following citations: "Only in mutual love, in which the concern of one person for the interests of another, prompts and elicits a reciprocal affection, are the social demands of historical existence satisfied." [37] "The Christian faith in its profoundest versions has never believed that the Cross would so change the very nature of historical existence that a more and more universal achievement of sacrificial

[34] *Nature and Destiny*, 2:69.

[35] *Christian Realism and Political Problems* (New York: Charles Scribner's Sons, 1953), p. 160. As the last two citations suggest, the terms "justice" and "harmony"—and now, by implication, "imperfect harmony"—appear to be, for the most part, Niebuhrian synonyms for "mutual love." It is true that Niebuhr's writings sometimes suggest distinctions between these terms. "The will to do justice is a form of love, for the interests of the neighbor are affirmed. Mutual love . . . is also a form of love, for the life of the other is enhanced" (ibid.). The distinction implicit here is probably that between reciprocity among a large number of individuals in a society (justice) and reciprocity among a small number of individuals, such as those included in family or friendship relations (mutual love). Several passages indicate that Niebuhr thinks the possibilities for "harmony with other interests and vitalities" (*Nature and Destiny*, 2:74) to be greater in the latter (see, e.g., *Faith and History*, p. 185). Insofar as "justice" and "mutual love" are reserved for these referents, "imperfect harmony" appears to be the inclusive term, indicating reciprocity whatever the number of individuals in question. But even if these distinctions are observed, all three terms are identical in this: each indicates an activity in which the self regards itself as an equal but not specially privileged member of a group. And it is this characteristic which, as we shall see, is critical to the argument which Niebuhr offers for his ethic. Consequently, we may, as he does more often than not, ignore the distinctions in question.

[36] *Nature and Destiny*, 2:247.

[37] Ibid., p. 69.

love would transmute sacrificial love into successful mutual love, perfectly validated and by historical social consequences."[38] If the "social demands of historical existence" require a reciprocal response to one's concern for another, and if only this successful mutuality provides validation by historical social consequences, it is plausible to conclude that historical social consequences "justify" a norm when they include the fulfillment of the agent's interests. This conclusion is strengthened when we note Niebuhr's claim that "non-Christian conceptions of love seek to justify love from the standpoint of the happiness of the agent"—or, what appears to be the same, that "mutual love, . . . seeks to relate life to life from the standpoint of the self and for the sake of the self's own happiness."[39] To take mutual love as the ultimate imperative, then, is to presume that the intended mutuality will be realized, so that the historical consequences of one's action will include one's own interest fulfillment. In short, mutual love is secularistic, for Niebuhr, because it assumes a coincidence of meaning (or, using the traditional ethical term, "virtue") and historical fulfillment; activity in obedience to the norm is assumed to be the activity which will maximize the satisfaction of one's own interests. It may be worth repeating at this point that Niebuhr does not intend to identify "mutual love" with "prudential self-interest." The point is not that the agent considers his or her concern for others to be simply instrumental. Rather, the agent intends the proportionate or reciprocal fulfillment of all relevant interests—and presumes that this mutuality will be realized, so that such action is coincident with his or her own satisfaction.

Nonetheless, just because mutual love presupposes such a coincidence, this ethical intention *inevitably* "degenerates from mutuality to a prudent regard for the interests of the self, and from an impulse toward community to an acceptance of the survival impulse as ethically normative"[40]—which is to say that this claim provides additional evidence that Niebuhr understands mutual love in the way we have described. It is this claim, of course, which allows him to say that "mutuality is not a possible achievement if it is made the intention and goal of action" and must, therefore, "be the unintended rather than purposed consequence."[41] But the important consideration here is

38 Ibid., p. 87.
39 Ibid., pp. 84, n. 16; 82.
40 Ibid., p. 96; see also p. 79; *Christian Realism*, p. 166.
41 *Nature and Destiny*, 2:69, 84.

Niebuhr's argument: Such degeneration is inevitable because the response of the other is unpredictable. Mutuality "is too uncertain a consequence to encourage the venture of life toward another," so that "actions are dominated by the fear that they may not be reciprocated." [42] If the intention of mutual love cannot be maintained because reciprocity is uncertain, the suppressed premise must be that this intention presupposes the guarantee of reciprocity. The agent will assume his action to be meaningful only if the intended mutuality inclusive of his own interest fulfillment is assured.

Secularism, we said earlier, is a conviction that the source of meaning is within the world—and, for Niebuhr, such a conviction is implicit in the presumption of "historical justification." Because a guarantee of the agent's historical fulfillment is the *sine qua non* of meaningful activity, Niebuhr reasons, the ultimate telos of mutual love must be a community within history—that is, some historical community made particular by the inclusion of just this historical fulfillment. Mutual love seeks historical "harmony with other human interests and vitalities"; the "strategies of mutual love" are those "in which the self, individual and collective, seeks to preserve its life and to relate it harmoniously to other lives." [43] And where the ultimate telos of activity is presumed to be within history, a historical or secularistic source of meaning is implied.

It is this affirmation of some particular historical community as the final goal of human activity which, Niebuhr argues, invalidates the ethic of mutual love. Historical possibilities, he claims, are indeterminate—and, therefore, no particular historical realization will suffice as the ultimate telos; no particular state of affairs can exhaust all possible value. "Harmony with other human interests and vitalities . . . is a desirable end of historical striving; but it can never be a final norm. For . . . all historical harmonies of interest [are] partial and incomplete." [44] Every historical achievement can be transcended or, to say the same, none can be perfect. "There are no limits to be set in history for the achievement of more inclusive brotherhood, for the development of more perfect and more inclusive mutual relations." [45] If it is asked how one knows that historical possibilities are indeterminate, Niebuhr answers that so much follows from the essential human

[42] Ibid., pp. 84, 69.
[43] Ibid., pp. 74, 96.
[44] Ibid., p. 74.
[45] Ibid., p. 85; see also p. 246.

capacity for self-transcendent freedom, the norm for which every ethic purports to give: "Man's freedom over the limits of nature in indeterminate regression means that no fixed limits can be placed upon either the purity or the breadth of the brotherhood for which men strive in history."[46] "In so far as . . . [man] has the freedom to transcend structure, standing beyond himself and every particular social situation, every law is subject to indeterminate possibilities which finally exceed the limits of any specific definition of what he 'ought' to do. Yet they do not stand completely outside of law, if law is defined in terms of man's essential nature. For this indeterminate freedom is a part of his essential nature."[47] The proper telos of human activity, therefore, must transcend history—that is, the source of meaning must be transcendent to the world: "[Man] transcends himself in such a way that he must choose his total end. In this task of self-determination he is confronted with endless potentialities and he can set no limit to what he ought to be, short of the character of ultimate reality."[48] "[Perfection] can neither be simply reduced to history nor yet dismissed because it transcends history. It transcends history as history transcends itself. It is the final norm of a human nature, which has no final norm in history because it is not contained in history."[49] It is this perfect community or state of affairs to which Niebuhr refers with the symbol "Kingdom of God" and which he variously describes as "perfect mutuality," "perfect brotherhood," "perfect harmony," and "the law of love."[50]

We are now in a position to return to the identity of sacrificial love and perfect harmony in Niebuhr's thought. Since the norm which affirms the self as equal but not specially privileged (i.e., mutual love) is secularistic, Niebuhr reasons, only complete disregard for self (i.e., sacrificial love) is conformity with a harmony transcendent to history. But if this is so, then the imperative to disregard self completely must follow from the meaning of "perfect harmony"—and Niebuhr believes that it does. As representing the indeterminate possibilities of human freedom, the argument runs, perfect harmony requires of each individual an indeterminate love which is compromised whenever the interests of the self are affirmed. This indeterminate love has, as we might put it, both intensive and extensive dimensions. Intensively,

[46] Ibid., p. 244.
[47] *Christian Realism*, pp. 154–55.
[48] *Nature and Destiny*, 1:163.
[49] Ibid., p. 75; see also *Pious and Secular*, p. 141.
[50] See, e.g., *Nature and Destiny*, 2:83, 85.

"there are no exact limits to the degree of imagination with which I may enter into the needs and consider the interests of the neighbor. The love commandment is therefore always a challenge which stands vertically over every moral act and achievement. It defines the dimension, ending in a transcendent Kingdom of God, in which all moral actions take place." [51] Because at some point the interests of the self will conflict with the needs and interests of the neighbor, attention to the former precludes indeterminate love for another person. "There is always the possibility of sacrificing our life and interest." [52] Extensively, perfect harmony calls for "a universal love which finite man is incapable of giving" and thus "can only be regarded as a reminder of the indeterminate possibilities which exist for man despite his finite and parochial loyalties." [53] Because an individual "can set no limit to what he ought to be short of the character of ultimate reality," [54] the admonition of Jesus, "'Be ye therefore perfect as your Father in heaven is perfect,'" means for Niebuhr, "'Let your love therefore be all-inclusive as God's love includes all.'" [55] But concern for the self insofar precludes attention to those whose interests conflict with one's own or those who will not reciprocate. "'If ye love them that love you, what thanks have ye?'" is, Niebuhr holds, the biblical expression of the fact that universal love is sacrificial. [56] In short, nothing less than indeterminate love, intensive and extensive, conforms to perfect brotherhood, and nothing less than complete disregard for self permits such perfect love.

In contrast to mutual love, then, the authentic norm denies the coincidence of meaning (or virtue) and historical fulfillment; it "dispenses with historical justification." [57] But one should not conclude from this that the law of love is not "justified." On the contrary, "the *agape*, the sacrificial love, which is for Christian faith revealed upon the Cross, has its primary justification in an 'essential reality' which transcends the realities of history, namely, the character of God." [58] Given the meaning of "historical justification," it seems fair to conclude

---

[51] "Common Life," p. 81.

[52] *Nature and Destiny*, 2:74–75; see also *Christian Realism*, p. 159.

[53] *Pious and Secular*, p. 122; see also p. 118.

[54] *Nature and Destiny*, 1:163.

[55] *Pious and Secular*, pp. 116–17.

[56] *Christian Realism*, p. 115; *Pious and Secular*, p. 118; "Common Life," p. 75.

[57] *Nature and Destiny*, 2:247.

[58] Ibid., p. 96.

that Niebuhr here means to assert a coincidence between authentic activity and *transcendent* fulfillment. Although one's interests may be sacrificed, precisely in sacrificial love one's life is genuinely fulfilled— for one is thereby authentically related to "the character of God." In other words, the biblical assurance that to lose one's life is to gain it means for Niebuhr that disregard for one's own interests is the purchase of one's true self or transcendent fulfillment. "Such a gain cannot be measured in terms of the history which is bound to nature. The gain can only be an integrity of spirit which has validity in 'eternity.' It can have meaning only when life is measured in a dimension which includes the fulfillment of life beyond the present conditions of history." [59]

Moreover, the coincidence with transcendent fulfillment may be explained through the identity of sacrificial love and perfect harmony. For perfect harmony is what Niebuhr means by the character (or Kingdom) of God—that is, authentic activity conforms to a state of affairs in which "all men are perfectly related to each other, because they are related in terms of perfect obedience and love to the center and source of their existence." [60] Although one's interests may be sacrificed, one is assured of transcendent fulfillment because the Kingdom of God is "the plane upon which all distinctions between mutual love and disinterested and sacrificing love vanish" [61]—is, in other words, a perfect mutuality. As a consequence, Niebuhr can affirm the "idea of a 'general resurrection,' in which all those who perished before the fulfillment of history, are brought back to participate in the final triumph," because it "does justice both to the value of the individual life, without which the fulfillment of history would be incomplete; and to the meaning of the whole course of history *for the individual*, without which his life cannot be fulfilled." [62] For Niebuhr, then, the norm of sacrificial love, which prohibits regard for the self, is the same as the norm of perfect harmony, which implies some self-affirmation, because the self which is disregarded is not the same as the

---

[59] Ibid., p. 75; see also *Faith and History*, pp. 175–76.

[60] *Beyond Tragedy*, p. 16.

[61] *Nature and Destiny*, 2:86.

[62] Ibid., p. 311, emphasis added; see also p. 36. We should note Niebuhr's insistence that this description is "implausible" when taken literally and must, therefore, be understood as "symbolically profound" (ibid., p. 311, n. 14). But this insistence does not change the fact that, for Niebuhr, the individual's life is fulfilled because the Kingdom of God is, in some sense, a perfect mutuality.

self which is affirmed. In the first instance, historical fulfillment is proscribed; in the second, transcendent fulfillment is assured.[63]

[63] It is probably important to consider a difficulty which awaits this reading of Niebuhr's ethic—namely, the implication that moral evil is consequent upon finitude. Logically speaking, indeterminate love is impossible for finite individuals. Of course, Niebuhr himself continually claims that "fulfillment of the law of love is no simple possibility" (ibid., 1:296) and, what is apparently the same, that this norm represents an "impossible possibility" (ibid., 2:76). But whether these statements should be understood to confirm the *logical* impossibility of moral obedience is open to dispute. For he also holds that humans inevitably misuse their freedom, and perhaps fulfillment of the law is "no simple possibility" for this reason. Indeed, the justly celebrated discussion of original sin in Niebuhr's Gifford Lectures labors to make clear that moral evil is *always* the misuse of freedom, the inevitability of that misuse notwithstanding (see ibid., vol. 1, chaps. 7–9). The relation of that discussion to Niebuhr's theistic ethic, however, is illumined by attention to his earlier writings. In the present context, I can only indicate my belief that, on the whole, earlier treatments understand wrongdoing to be not only the misuse of freedom but also consequent upon finitude—and that precisely because the law of love is impossible (see *An Interpretation of Christian Ethics* [New York: Harper & Bros., 1935; Living Age Books Edition, New York: Meridian Books, 1956], pp. 66–67; "Common Life," pp. 72–79, 94–95; "Religion and Action," pp. 46–49). To be sure, the documentation of this claim would not alter the fact that Niebuhr's considered or mature position on the matter is presented in his Gifford Lectures. It is equally beyond question that the reason for this change of mind is Niebuhr's intent so to understand moral failure as to preclude the implication that God is responsible for evil—or, what comes to the same thing, that theism is properly classical. Nonetheless, the earlier treatments are significant because, notwithstanding the subsequent changes in his understanding of wrongdoing, there is no substantial indication that Niebuhr's ethic changes correspondingly. On the contrary, I have argued, only if the indeterminate demand of that ethic is maintained can one make sense of the identity between perfect harmony and sacrificial love which pervades the Gifford Lectures themselves. And, in subsequent writings, the indeterminate ethic is either explicitly affirmed or clearly implied (see, e.g., *Pious and Secular*, p. 122; *Faith and History*, p. 179; *Christian Realism*, pp. 154–55; "Reply to Interpretation and Criticism," in *Reinhold Niebuhr: His Religious, Social, and Political Thought*, ed. Charles W. Kegley and Robert W. Bretall [New York: Macmillan Co., 1956], p. 434). Moreover, Niebuhr appears to leave his ethic unaltered for the same reason that his understanding of sin is changed—namely, that each is, he believes, required by authentic theism. Just as his religious conviction is incompatible with necessary sin, so the same theism, he believes, requires an ultimate imperative to which historical activity can never completely conform. There is substantial reason to think, I am suggesting, that its inconsistency with his mature doctrine of evil does not count against the reading of Niebuhr's ethic offered here. Rather, this inconsistency can be understood in terms of the development of Niebuhr's systematic thought. It is the consequence of his attempt to correct an error which he perceived in his earlier position without sacrificing what he held to be essential to a theistic ethic. Either he is not aware of the resulting dilemma or, what is far more likely, he sees no way to resolve it. One merit of this reading is that it suggests at least one reason for the puzzle *within* Niebuhr's mature understanding of sin—i.e., his insistence upon the inevitability of what is nothing other than the misuse of freedom. To relinquish the inescapable character of sin would be to deny that moral obedience is historically impossible, and that, for Niebuhr, would be a compromise of his

III

If the preceding discussion gives reason to believe that Niebuhr's understanding of "perfect harmony" is such as to imply "sacrificial love," then we also have reason to doubt whether he has succeeded in formulating the ethic of authentic theism. Since authentic theism affirms a source of meaning *inclusive of history*, the ethic of authentic theism must include (though, clearly, not be exhausted by) an affirmation of the self's historical fulfillment. But precisely this affirmation is excluded by the imperative to disregard one's self-interest completely.

The point may be rephrased. Niebuhr holds, we may recall, that secularistic ethics should be rejected because they require the pursuit of some historical telos, and classical ethics should be rejected because they require some nonhistorical activity ("escape from history").[64] Assuming, with Niebuhr, that only authentic theism remains among the logical alternatives, it follows that authentic theism requires a historical activity in pursuit of a nonhistorical telos. Niebuhr further holds that the nonhistorical telos in question implies the imperative to disregard one's self-interest completely. If this is the case, the transcendent telos must be exclusive of the self's historical fulfillment. Moreover, since the theistic alternatives (i.e., classicism and authentic theism) are distinguished by the exclusion or inclusion of history *as such*, sacrificial love is implied only if the telos is exclusive of history. But this last contradicts the call for a historical activity.

Just because Niebuhr's understanding of perfect harmony does imply sacrificial love, in other words, one is led to the conclusion that his theistic ethic is, in his own terms, implicitly classical rather than authentic. This does not mean to say that Niebuhr intends such a position. On the contrary, he identifies the two norms because he believes such to be required by authentic theism. The argument here means to say that Niebuhr's formulation of the ultimate imperative violates his own intentions (i.e., is *implicitly* classical)—so that his theistic ethic is, in that respect, internally inconsistent.[65]

---

theistic ethic. While theism cannot be authentic unless humans are responsible for their wrongdoing, ethics is not theistic unless moral failure is "inevitable."

[64] See above.

[65] For the sake of clarity, it is worth noting another problem involved in Niebuhr's identification of *agape* and perfect harmony. Let us grant that indeterminate love implies disregard for self—i.e., that "the final goodness. . . stands in contradiction to all forms of human goodness in which self-assertion and love are compounded" (*Nature and Destiny*, 2:89). There is, then, an illicit conversion involved when Niebuhr concludes that *agape* implies indeterminate love, i.e., that "sacrificial love seeks

Niebuhr's formulation fails to fulfill his intentions, I suggest, because his ethical reasoning includes an illicit deduction. Having argued that the indeterminate possibilities of history require a transcendent telos (i.e., perfect harmony), he further claims that this telos requires an indeterminate love of which every affirmation of self-interest is a compromise (i.e., implies the imperative of sacrificial love.) [66] But this last claim involves a non sequitur. It overlooks—and, therefore, unwittingly collapses—the distinction between an *ideal to be pursued* and an *ideal to be illustrated*. It is one thing to say that perfect harmony should be pursued; it is quite another to say that this ideal should be illustrated.

The distinction in question should be clarified. An ideal to be pursued defines the proper end of activity; an ideal to be illustrated defines the proper character of activity. The two may well be related; the proper character of activity may be defined as the pursuit of some specified end. Because the character is defined as *pursuit* of the end, however, this simply confirms that the ideal to be pursued and the ideal to be illustrated are not necessarily the same. Let us suppose, for instance, that one believes world peace—understood, say, as mutual trust and respect among the nations—to be a proper end of activity. Accordingly, present activity should seek to promote such a state of affairs. World peace is the ideal to be pursued; the pursuit of world peace is the ideal to be illustrated. It is, then, quite another thing to hold that one should be a pacifist—to hold that peacefulness is the

---

conformity with, . . . , the ultimate and final harmony of life with life" (ibid., p. 81)— unless, of course, "regard for self" or "self-assertion" changes meaning as one moves from the first statement to the second. When *agape* is defined in contrast to mutual love, self-assertion is taken to mean concern for one's own happiness or self-interest. While such concern is incompatible with indeterminate love, the same is true of any particular or limited concern. One may well disregard one's own happiness and yet not love indeterminately—e.g., one may be solely concerned with the self-interests of *some* others. Action incompatible with perfect harmony is necessarily "self-assertion," then, only if this term now means simply that particularity of attention which any human activity necessarily illustrates. Thus, if Niebuhr's norm of perfect harmony is said to include the norm of *agape*, the former is not thereby exhausted. It may be that Niebuhr at least senses this problem. Perhaps his occasional suggestion, noted earlier, that *agape* is "ecstatic" in a sense to which thinking is alien indicates a tendency so to escalate the meaning of "sacrificial love" as to make it equivalent to "indeterminate love." For deliberation, to Niebuhr, implies the calculation necessary to adjudicate the conflicts between interests (a necessity in this world even if the agent excludes his own interests from consideration). In the Kingdom of God, as Niebuhr understands it, no such calculation would be required.

[66] See above.

proper character of activity or the ideal to be illustrated. We may grant that in some situations peacefulness may be the best way to promote mutual trust and respect. But that is a further decision requiring further deliberation—and is not, therefore, simply another way of saying that peace is the end of one's activity. Consequently, Niebuhr himself argues with considerable determination that pacifism may well be destructive of peace among the nations (e.g., in response to a nation such as Nazi Germany).[67]

To pursue the example, let us suppose that someone committed to the pursuit of world peace neglects the distinction between an ideal to be pursued and an ideal to be illustrated. From the premise that world peace is the proper end, he or she would then conclude that we should always act as if there were peaceful mutuality (i.e., should be pacifist)— so that pacifism is understood as an activity illustrating this ideal state of affairs. Similarly, when Niebuhr argues that the indeterminate possibilities of history require a transcendent telos, he defends perfect harmony as an ideal to be pursued; but when he further claims that perfect harmony requires indeterminate (and, therefore, sacrificial) love, he transforms the ultimate telos into an ideal to be illustrated. For indeterminate love, as Niebuhr understands it, is an activity wherein one acts as if the Kingdom of God were realized—that is, illustrates such a state of affairs. From the premise that the Kingdom of God is the proper end, Niebuhr improperly concludes that this Kingdom is normative for character. "[Man] transcends himself in such a way that he must choose his total *end*. In this task of self-determination he is confronted with endless potentialities and he can set no limit to what he *ought to be*, short of the character of ultimate reality."[68]

As this critique suggests, a similar problem seems to be involved in Niebuhr's appeal to the indeterminate possibilities of human existence. From the premise of human freedom, it is one thing to conclude that "the achievements of justice in history may rise in indeterminate degrees to find their fulfillment in a more perfect love and brotherhood"[69]—so that "no fixed limits can be placed upon the purity or the

---

[67] See, e.g., *Power Politics*, chap. 1.

[68] *Nature and Destiny*, 1:163; emphasis added. One may also note the following citation: "His [Jesus'] ethical doctrine contains an uncompromising insistence upon conformity to God's will without reference to the relativities and contingencies of historical situations" (ibid., 2:73). If conformity to God's will were the pursuit of a transcendent end, it would not ignore "reference to the relativities and contingencies of historical situations."

[69] Ibid., 2:246; see also p. 85.

breadth of the brotherhood"[70] which humans in some distant future might realize. As an ideal representative of human freedom, then, perfect harmony or perfect brotherhood is a transcendent end. It is quite another thing, however, to assert that human freedom yields indeterminate possibilities for any given activity or any given individual. "The love universalism of the gospels . . . demands a universal love which finite man is incapable of giving. It can only be regarded as a reminder of the indeterminate possibilities of freedom which exist for man despite his finite and parochial loyalties."[71] "In so far as man has a determinate structure, it is possible to state the 'essential nature' of human existence to which his actions ought to conform and which they should fulfill. But in so far as he has the freedom to transcend structure, standing beyond himself and every particular social situation, every law is subject to indeterminate possibilities which finally exceed any specific definition of what he 'ought' to do. Yet they do not stand completely outside of law, if law is defined in terms of man's essential nature. For this indeterminate freedom is a part of his essential nature."[72] Niebuhr's apparent failure to distinguish clearly the second meaning of "indeterminate" from the first reflects his transformation of the ideal to be pursued into an ideal to be illustrated.

Since this transformation makes possible the identity of perfect harmony and sacrificial love in Niebuhr's ethic, one has reason to ask whether Niebuhr's argument against the norm of mutual love is sound. Mutual love is inherently secularistic, Niebuhr holds, because it presupposes the coincidence of meaning (or virtue) and historical fulfillment. On the face of it, this assertion seems peculiar. There seems to be no reason why one who seeks to satisfy "all claims within the general field of interests proportionately"[73] must presume a guarantee that his or her interests will be fulfilled. Indeed, this presumption is inconsistent with such activity—and that for reasons which Niebuhr himself gives: the actions and reactions of others are in some measure unpredictable. In addition, self-interests conflict, and it may be the case that proportionate regard for all is best served by a relative denial of one's own. Niebuhr is quite right, then, in saying that mutuality cannot be achieved if the coincidence in question is assumed, that this assumption causes activity to "degenerate" into "prudential

70 Ibid., p. 244.
71 *Pious and Secular*, p. 122.
72 *Christian Realism*, pp. 154–55; see also *Nature and Destiny*, 2:170.
73 *Nature and Destiny*, 2:69.

self-interest." Therefore, it is also quite right to say that one must be *willing* to sacrifice one's own interests. "Love, heedless of self, must be the initiator of any reciprocal love"[74] is, *in this sense*, correct. And if the equal regard commanded is universalized, so that all present and future individuals are included, sacrifice may be a frequent consequence of obedience, and the grounds upon which one is willing to give up the fulfillment of one's own interests may become a pressing matter in ethical theory. All of this does not mean, however, as Niebuhr believes it does, that "mutuality is not a possible achievement if it is made the intention and goal of any action."[75] On the contrary, what follows is that the intention and goal of mutuality denies the coincidence of meaning and interest fulfillment. Moreover, if the equal regard is indeed universalized—such that the aim in question may be defined as maximal mutuality and, by implication, in the long run—then it might well be argued that mutual love is theistic in presupposition. And the argument might call upon the very consideration which Niebuhr urges against secularistic ethics—namely, that every historical achievement can be transcended. "There are no limits to be set in history for the achievement of more perfect and more inclusive mutual relations."[76]

To suggest that Niebuhr implicitly affirms the theistic entailment of mutual love leads one to ask why he explicitly denies it. A possible explanation may be indicated by Niebuhr's erroneous transformation of the ideal to be pursued into an ideal to be illustrated. Whatever may be the logic of his argument, Niebuhr's neglect of this distinction may reveal that his thought begins in fact with the norm of indeterminate love, with the conviction that perfect mutuality must be illustrated in activity. Because he is already convinced that authentic theism calls for sacrificial love, in other words, Niebuhr concludes that mutual love must be secularistic. Similarly, then, we could give some account of his peculiar claim that mutual love presupposes the coincidence of meaning and historical fulfillment. If he is already persuaded that sacrificial love is the purchase of one's true self, then he

74 "Reply to Interpretation and Criticism," p. 442.

75 *Nature and Destiny*, 2:69.

76 Ibid. To argue in this way is to suggest my indebtedness to the discussion of Niebuhr's ethic and the constructive alternative offered by Daniel Day Williams in his volume, *God's Grace and Man's Hope* (see pp. 73–78). What Williams's discussion does not explain, however, is why Niebuhr identifies the norms of sacrificial love and perfect harmony. To put the matter in my terms, Williams does not explain Niebuhr's transformation of the ideal to be pursued into an ideal to be illustrated.

might well conclude that mutual love presumes the guarantee of a "false" self—presumes that one's interests will be satisfied.

If this explanation has merit, however, it also raises another question—namely, why does Niebuhr, in his understanding of the ultimate imperative, collapse the distinction between an ideal to be pursued and an ideal to be illustrated? This question is all the more appropriate since we have already mentioned in passing his polemic against pacifism—for this suggests his awareness of a distinction between pursuing and illustrating something like "world peace." Moreover, it might be noted that this polemic is simply a specification of Niebuhr's belief that conditions of higher justice are always something unrealized in history and, therefore, something to be *pursued*. To note this, however, suggests a reason for Niebuhr's failure to apply the same distinction to transcendent reality. If the distinction applies within history because conditions of higher justice remain unrealized, the collapse may indicate that Niebuhr understands transcendent reality to be without unrealized states of affairs. Although the present context prohibits a pursuit of this hypothesis, I might simply assert my belief that extended discussion would bear it out—would confirm that, for Niebuhr, the Kingdom of God is, always has been, and always will be transcendently realized. More precisely put, perhaps, Niebuhr holds the distinctions between past, present, and future to be inapplicable to divinity. In saying this, I do not for a moment intend to deny that the inclusion of history within the divine is utterly fundamental to Niebuhr's position. Rather, I mean to say that his vision of the God who includes the world is finally determined by the traditional assumption that divinity itself is not temporal; for Niebuhr, "eternity" is the inclusive characterization of God. Just because he believes any compromise of this claim to be a compromise of authentic theism, Niebuhr's ethic is implicitly classical. And, if this is so, it suggests that such a claim is not in fact essential to authentic theism but is, on the contrary, itself classical by implication.

In any case, our conclusions regarding Niebuhr's theistic ethic give reason to doubt whether that ethic may serve his attempt to relate theism and political theory. For classical theism, as Niebuhr defines it, denies the meaning of politics. Having noted that consequence, it is perhaps important to say again that Niebuhr's intention is unequivocally to the contrary. There can be no question that Niebuhr intends, as we noted at the outset, so to understand politics in particular and history in general as to affirm both their meaning and their theistic source. The argument here is simply that his formulation of the ultimate imperative violates just that intention.[77] And there is, it seems to me, no more telling evidence for the reading of his ethic offered here than Niebuhr's preoccupation with the "application" of the ultimate imperative to political activity, or, as he also puts it, the relation of "Christ's perfection" to history.[78] The pivotal chapter of his early systematic work is entitled "The Relevance of an Impossible Ethical Ideal,"[79] and he writes, in the 1950s, "There is, in short, no social ethic in the love universalism of the gospels,"[80] so that "the problem of the application of the law of love to the collective relationships of mankind contains within itself the whole possibility of a Christian social ethic."[81] It is, I am suggesting, precisely because his ethic is implicitly classical that the question of its relevance to political activity is, for Niebuhr, continually problematic.

We may summarize by noting that what has been said does not necessarily show that Niebuhr's ethic should be rejected. For the principal argument of this essay has sought to demonstrate that Niebuhr's understanding of the ultimate imperative is, *in his own terms*, inadequate. Since it is his distinction between classicism and authentic theism which informs the critique offered here, the main line of discussion has simply attempted to document an internal contradiction in Niebuhr's thought—or, to be repetitious, to show that his ethic

[77] Given Niebuhr's intention, it is not surprising that he frequently argues for a distinction between his ethic and those of classicism. "It will be noted that the Christian statement of the ideal possibility does not involve self-negation but self-realization. The self is, in other words, not evil by reason of being a particular self and its salvation does not consist in absorption into the eternal. Neither is the self divided, as in Hegelianism, into a particular or empirical and a universal self; and salvation does not consist in sloughing off its particularity and achieving universality" (*Nature and Destiny*, 1:251). Or, again: "The Christian ethical norm has little relation to mystical concepts according to which the particularity of egohood is regarded as an evil and redemption is equated with the absorption of individual consciousness into universal consciousness. In contrast to such schemes of redemption from self, the Christian faith does promise self-realization" (*Faith and History*, p. 175). These assertions do not, however, mitigate the force of our conclusion. If the particularity of egohood is not regarded as an evil, then the ethical demand of complete disregard for self must be qualified. If one's salvation does not consist in sloughing off particularity, then the ultimate imperative calls for something less than indeterminate love. Citations such as the above, I suggest, merely indicate again the inconsistency between Niebuhr's intention and the formulation of his theistic ethic.

[78] *Nature and Destiny*, 2:76.

[79] *Christian Ethics*, p. 97.

[80] *Pious and Secular*, p. 118.

[81] "Christian Faith and Social Action," in *Christian Faith and Social Action*, ed. John H. Hutchison (New York: Charles Scribner's Sons, 1953), p. 237.

violates his own intention. From which it follows that only those who affirm Niebuhr's intention, who affirm his understanding and refutation of secularism and classicism, are logically compelled to reject his ethic.

As the reader may have surmised, however, I find Niebuhr's understanding and refutation of secularism and classicism persuasive. I cannot present here the reasons for this judgment. But it provides the basis of my conviction that a contemporary attempt to respond to the challenge of secularism and to provide a positive interpretation of political life cannot appropriate Niebuhr's ethic without whatever revision is required to purge it of classical implications. On the other hand, the same judgment leads me to conclude that Niebuhr's enterprise moves us a considerable way toward an adequate formulation. For I have said that he presents a convincing *negative* argument for the meaning of politics and for its theistic source. Through that argument alone, in my judgment, Niebuhr enjoys considerable success in his attempt to relate theism and political theory.

Realism, Radicalism, and Eschatology in Reinhold Niebuhr: A Reassessment

Roger L. Shinn

Ours is a time of shifting vogues of thought. The themes that stir excitement soon become targets of criticism, or, worse, turn simply passé. Intellectual heroes come and go quickly. In such a milieu it is not surprising that criticism often goes full circle: people and ideas are acclaimed, rejected, and rediscovered in breathless haste.

No wonder, then, that Reinhold Niebuhr means different things to different people. Some, deeply disaffected with American society and skeptical that this nation can solve its moral and political problems, respond to Niebuhr as the semi-Marxist and the polemical critic of "liberalism." Others, living through the quick rise and fall of the recent New Left, see in Niebuhr the "tamed cynic" and the critic of romanticism in politics.

The reassessment of Niebuhr cannot be a static enterprise. A thinker always on the move, he continuously responded to criticisms, including his own trenchant self-criticisms. To evaluate his ideas in his presence was always to enter into dialogue with him, awaiting the next reply. His thought was vibrant enough that the dialogue will continue, in the sense that dialogue often continues with thinkers of the past. This essay is a contribution to such dialogue. It centers on familiar themes in the political thought and theology of Niebuhr: on utopianism and realism, on radicalism and pragmatism, on eschatalogy and political activity.

I. UTOPIANISM AND REALISM

Reinhold Niebuhr was a spirited polemicist, and he built a reputation as a scourge of utopians. Today much of mankind is more frustrated and less confident of the future than during most of Niebuhr's career. Yet there are signs of a new utopianism—a tenuous utopianism, sometimes frail and sometimes ardent, often precariously raised up out of the midst of despair, but nonetheless alive. The utopian yearning is immensely varied. It includes the cosmic optimism of Teilhard de Chardin, the exuberant secularism of Harvey Cox in one mood and the festive religious celebration of the same Harvey Cox in a later mood, the briefly conspicuous "worldly optimism" of William Hamilton, the theologies of hope with their mingling of Marxist certitude and Christian eschatology, and those strains in the youth culture that dream of noncompetitive communal life and world peace.

To mention these is to indicate how fragile they are, how briefly most of them moved through their crescendo and decrescendo. Anti-utopias are more prominent in literature, drama, and film than utopias. Nevertheless, the utopian spirit still lives—whether bravely, foolishly, or wistfully.

Anybody who attacks utopia bears a certain burden of proof. Who can object to hoping for a better future? Why should not mankind envision ideal futures toward which people may aspire, perhaps improving life even though they never attain their visions? Utopias might be judged at best creative, at worst harmless. Skeptics can always leave them alone. Only a crabbed personality, some would say, would go to the trouble of attacking them.

If we ask why Reinhold Niebuhr assaulted utopianism, we must investigate what it was that he actually attacked. He was no enemy of transcendent vision. Prophecy and eschatology were at the heart of his theology. Yet he insisted on what he called "realism" as against utopianism. In his battles against "the children of darkness" he was not willing to join unequivocally "the children of light." Everybody knew that Niebuhr opposed tyranny, exploitation, and oppression. But everybody felt also his scorn for naiveté, sentimentalism, and all those hopes that did not take into account the tragic qualities of history or the sin in the human heart.

At various stages of his career, Niebuhr made certain affirmations of human possibilities and aspirations. Three examples are notable.

In his first major book, *Moral Man and Immoral Society* (*1932*), he quoted Shelley's Prometheus, advocating

> hope, till hope creates
> From its own wreck the thing it contemplates.

He continued: "An optimistic appraisal of human potentialities may therefore create its own verification." It will surprise no one who knew Niebuhr that the next sentence starts with the word "but" and that he went on to warn: "Human beings are endowed by nature with both selfish and unselfish impulses."[1] If he often reminded liberal culture of the former, he did not forget the latter.

A decade later in the Gifford Lectures on "The Nature and Destiny of Man," he established his reputation as the unveiler par excellence of human sin in its blatant and subtle forms. Somehow it is often forgotten, by those who call him a neoorthodox or neo-Reformation theologian, that volume 2 called for a synthesis of Reformation and Renaissance. The Reformation, he said, saw "the ultimate answer of grace to the problem of guilt," but "it did not illumine the possibilities and limits of realizing increasing truth and goodness in every conceivable historic and social situation."[2] Hence, we must learn from the Renaissance "that life in history" is "filled with indeterminate possibilities," that in political life men always "face new possibilities of the good and the obligation to realize them,"[3] even while we remember that all human achievements are corruptible.

His book of 1965, *Man's Nature and His Communities*, in assigning a somewhat higher regard than heretofore to man's self-fulfilling impulse and even to human ambition as a component of creativity, showed the influence of his long friendship with Erik Erikson.[4] Its discussion of "Man's Tribalism as One Source of His Humanity" characteristically pointed out how human loyalties are corrupted by parochial loyalties. But the longest chapter, in its analysis of "Idealist and Realist Political Theories," argued the inadequacy of any political understanding that neglects either man's higher aspirations or his self-interested ideological taint. Interestingly, he made a criticism of Hans Morgenthau's "political realism," which is often regarded as similar to Niebuhr's, as insufficiently aware of the "residual force" of man's higher loyalties,

[1] Reinhold Niebuhr, *Moral Man and Immoral Society* (New York: Charles Scribner's Sons, 1932), p. 25. This book ends by paying a qualified tribute to the "valuable illusion" that "the collective life of mankind can achieve perfect justice." Niebuhr finds that illusion "dangerous because it encourages terrible fanaticisms," yet necessary for the achievement of approximations to justice (p. 277). In later years, his critics often quoted this paragraph back to him, and he usually replied by dismissing it as an error of his immaturity.

[2] Reinhold Niebuhr, *The Nature and Destiny of Man*, vol. 2, *Human Destiny* (New York: Charles Scribner's Sons, 1943), pp. 204–5.

[3] Ibid., p. 207.

[4] Reinhold Niebuhr, *Man's Nature and His Communities* (New York: Charles Scribner's Sons: 1965). Erikson is specifically mentioned on p. 109. The Preface uses Erikson's language of "basic trust," in quotation marks but without a citation.

87

even when they are corrupted.[5] And in a characteristic self-criticism, he looked back on "my rather violent, and sometimes extravagant, reaction to what I defined as the 'utopianism,' i.e., the illusory idealist and individualist character of a Protestant and bourgeois culture before the world depression and two world wars."[6]

In each of these cases the familiar dialectic calls attention to human nobility in its intermingling with the anxieties that underlie the lethargy or pride that betray nobility. In both its central structure and its nuances the dialectic is carefully balanced. Yet the overwhelming impression that Niebuhr made was that of a polemicist—consistent, sharp, and unrelenting—against utopianism. We must ask why.

In part, the reason was cultural. When Niebuhr pointed to the higher possibilities of human nature—the "original righteousness" and the workings of grace in human life—people heard themes familiar in their culture and were not surprised or jolted. When he insisted on the persistence and ubiquity of sin, the message was an affront to the liberal culture that felt its sting. Perhaps for the same reasons there was a peculiar passion in the attacks on optimistic illusions. Niebuhr thought that utopia was in error because it ignored the reality of sin. He also thought it was disastrous in its political consequences.

Niebuhr's clearest explanation of the harmful consequences of utopianism is in one of his less conspicuous writings, an editorial in *Christianity and Society* (Autumn 1947) called "Two Forms of Utopianism." The theme is stated in two sentences: "Hard utopianism might be defined as the creed of those who claim to embody the perfect community and who therefore feel themselves morally justified in using every instrument of guile or force against those who oppose their assumed perfection. Soft utopianism is the creed of those who do not claim to embody perfection, but expect perfection to emerge out of the ongoing process of history."[7]

Hard utopianism found its most obvious example in Stalinist communism, which justified cruelty in the name of its moral goals. This theme was made familiar, not only by Niebuhr, but by Arthur Koestler, Albert Camus, and many another. Hard utopianism justified

[5] Ibid., pp. 75–76. Niebuhr and Morgenthau, though friends and allies in many causes, were open in expressing their differences.

[6] *Man's Nature and His Communities*, p. 21.

[7] Reinhold Niebuhr, "Two Forms of Utopianism," *Christianity and Society* 12, no. 4 (Autumn 1947): 6. *Christianity and Society*, the quarterly publication of the Fellowship of Socialist Christians, edited by Reinhold Niebuhr, should not be confused with *Christianity and Crisis*, the bi-weekly with a wider circulation.

slaughter for the sake of the utopia that rarely or never arrived. Its moral need was for some humility, some self-awareness that would refrain from absolutizing its own good against the enemy's evil.

A more recent example might be the official U.S. apologetic for the recent ventures in Asia. By this time there is little utopianism in the national morale; there is, rather, a general recognition that this country recently waged the most dreary and sordid war of its history. The nation has almost forgotten the homilies of Lyndon Johnson and Dean Rusk—and of Richard Nixon and Spiro Agnew. The hard utopian ideology was that we were fighting to protect the cause of freedom against aggression, to vindicate democracy, to make credible our readiness to defend free peoples. This was represented as the one last struggle to preserve the good embodied in the free world against its potential destroyers.

Soft utopianism, in Niebuhr's judgment, was not cruel but was sentimental and irrelevant. At one time it was represented by those who hailed the Kellogg-Briand Peace Pact in eschatological enthusiasm—it is hard to realize today what store was set by that rhetorical renunciation of war—with no realization of the hard political and economic struggles that were simultaneously leading toward war. It was more immediately represented, in Niebuhr's editorial, by those who "are still dreaming of creating an ideal world government without answering the question of how we could beguile the Russians into accepting its authority, or for that matter, how it could get past the United States Senate." It is the theme of those who, like Billy Graham, would overcome racial injustice by redeeming the hearts of men—again with no awareness of the tough institutional structures and conflicts of power that entrap the hearts of men.

We might today examine the two utopian themes in President Nixon. It is too much to expect a consistent political philosophy, to say nothing of a consistent utopianism, in Nixon. Yet his utopian rhetoric has swung in both directions—hard and soft. To C. L. Sulzberger of the *New York Times*, Nixon said on March 8, 1971: "This war is ending. In fact, I seriously doubt if we will ever have another war. This is very probably the very last one."[8] What does such language mean? There is the strain of hard utopianism: a president, identifying himself as "a devoted pacifist," says that we will move to peace by whipping the Vietcong. But a curious element of soft utopianism pervades the

[8] Richard Nixon, interviewed by C. L. Sulzberger, *New York Times*, March 10, 1971, p. 14.

same interview. War—not simply this war but all war—is about to end. How? By good intentions? By what political and economic structures? By what adjudication of conflicting claims of Egyptians and Israelis, Indians and Pakistanis, North Americans and Latin Americans, Russians and Chinese? By what changes in relations between rich and poor nations? By what answers to population and starvation and disproportionate power? Such questions are simply lost in a hopefulness that somehow the conflicts that make for war are ending.

It is a long way from Nixon to the New Left—or, as we almost have to say now, with some regret, the old New Left. Surely it was utopian. It yearned for a world of spontaneous cooperation, unchained by the power structures and power conflicts that bedeviled the world of the establishment. Was its utopianism hard or soft? In fact, it split both ways. Its hard utopians were the militants who became elitist cadres, amateur demolitions specialists, and tough rioters. Its soft utopians expected corporations and governments to melt under a "new politics," then when a "children's crusade" did not succeed, often retired into mysticism, astrology, or isolated communes. When something better has come out of the New Left, often its style is aspiration without utopian expectation.

A final example is evident in the technocratic dreams of our time. Again the utopianism turns both ways. The soft utopians expect cybernation to relieve men of work and offer affluent leisure, untroubled by the deep conflicts of power over the control of the new machines. The hard utopians call on technological elites to take charge and establish compulsory control of the economy, education, genetics, the right of reproduction, and personality-shaping drugs.

Niebuhr, though the critic of utopia, entered into social conflict to correct wrongs and strive for approximations of justice. Unlike the soft utopians, he did so by seeking to deal with distribution of power; unlike hard utopians he constantly warned against the abuses of power even by the best-intentioned. Long before the coinage of the slogan "Black Power," Niebuhr worked with the basic idea. "However large the number of individual white men who do and who will identify themselves completely with the Negro cause, the white race in America will not admit the Negro to equal rights if it is not forced to do so. Upon that point one may speak with a dogmatism which all history justifies."[9] It is doubtful that anyone is left whose utopianism on that

9 *Moral Man and Immoral Society*, p. 253.

issue is unchastened by the events of the four decades following that statement.

II. RADICALISM AND PRAGMATISM

The same issues arise in a somewhat different way when we examine the role of pragmatism in Niebuhr's thought. During his career he moved from what he came to consider a too doctrinaire political philosophy to a more pragmatic one. It was a move from a socialism, quite polemical toward efforts of the New Deal to repair and reform a failing capitalism, to support of Franklin D. Roosevelt and the New Deal.

Niebuhr was never an unmitigated pragmatist. His was a pragmatism in a theological context, a pragmatism suffused with the doctrine of sin and tragedy, a pragmatism concerned to find proximate solutions to humanly insoluble problems. At the center of his theology was the cross of Christ, and he deeply resented any effort to interpret the cross pragmatically as a calculated device for achieving historical goals. But in the area of political ethics he repeatedly attacked dogmatic ideologies and asked for empirical and pragmatic assessment of actual possibilities.

The paradox of pragmatism is that it is an avowedly progressive philosophy that in the last analysis may be conservative. In the familiar formulations of William James and John Dewey, a pragmatic ethic is inherently progressive because it looks not to past authority but to future possibilities, not to precedents but to consequences. Yet as Eduard Heimann often argued against Niebuhr, pragmatism presupposes a general consensus about society and its goals.[10] In asking its favorite question—"what works?"—pragmatism asks the question within a context. Obviously what works within one context may not work within another, and pragmatism assumes a context. The context is usually a functioning social system, in need of improvement, but capable of improvement. The context includes also some kind of consensus on values. John Dewey, for example, despite all his insistence on questioning the authority of inherited standards, was confident that "the validity of justice, affection, and . . . truth" is "assured in

[10] Eduard Heimann, an economist and lay theologian, had been a close friend of Paul Tillich in the German Religious Socialist movement. Coming to America, he taught for years in the graduate faculty of the New School for Social Research. His cooperation and running argument with Niebuhr took place in the Fellowship of Socialist Christians (later the Frontier Fellowship). One statement of his argument may be found in his essay, "Niebuhr's Pragmatic Conservatism," *Union Seminary Quarterly Review*, vol. 11, no. 4 (May 1956).

its hold upon humanity."[11] A radical revolutionary ethic may begin by questioning the very values that Dewey thought securely established. The conservatism of pragmatism is in what it takes for granted. Niebuhr, because he emphasized the "offense" of the Christian gospel and of "the foolishness of God," was less inclined than secular pragmatists to take ethical assumptions for granted. But by his repeated declaration, he became increasingly pragmatic in political ethics.

For a long time the fashionable criticism of Reinhold Niebuhr was to ask why he took so long to become a pragmatist. This was the criticism of Arthur Schlesinger, Jr., who admired Niebuhr but thought him slow in coming to appreciate pragmatism. Niebuhr's response was to acknowledge his slowness.[12] Pragmatism meant to him the triumph over abstract doctrine. It was empirical and flexible. It abandoned rhetoric for acts that made a difference.

Today, in the irony of history, exactly the reverse criticism of Niebuhr is popular. Eduard Heimann was in this regard a forerunner. Now many critics of society have taken up the theme. Pragmatism, to them, means working within the system, making peace with the establishment, capitulating to the going ethic. Pragmatism justifies basic acceptance of the status quo as against revolution. For evidence, they say, look at Daniel Bell's description of *The End of Ideology*. Look at John F. Kennedy's praise of pragmatism as against ideology, then at how he gathered into his government the Ivy League experts who led us into the morass in Southeast Asia. Look at Arthur Schlesinger's years in the White House. Look at Hubert Humphrey, Reinhold Niebuhr's old friend in the Americans for Democratic Action, who pragmatically accommodated to the role of vice-president.

Some of the corresponding criticisms of Niebuhr are manifestly unfair. As I read some, I would never guess that he was, within the limits of his failing physical strength, one of the nation's most vociferous critics of the war in Indochina. If he was an apologist for the establishment, that is news to the Johnson and Nixon administrations. If he neglected the *theologia crucis* for pragmatic accommodation, that is news to all who know his theology. Ronald Stone has reported that when a hundred seminary students, in Holy Week of 1971, protested

[11] John Dewey, *A Common Faith* (New Haven, Conn.: Yale University Press, 1934).

[12] Arthur J. Schlesinger, Jr., "Reinhold Niebuhr's Role in American Political Thought and Life," in *Reinhold Niebuhr: His Religious, Social, and Political Thought*, ed. Charles W. Kegley and Robert W. Bretall (New York: Macmillan Co., 1956), pp. 125–50. For Niebuhr's response, see his "Reply to Interpretation and Criticism" in the same book, p. 436.

against the war in Vietnam, they took with them to prison more books by Niebuhr than by any other writer.[13]

But there is a point in the questioning of pragmatism. If politics is the art of the possible, who will aspire to the impossible? And if no one tries for the impossible, how will we know the limits of the possible? Does the art of the possible presuppose the persistence of reigning institutions and ideologies? Not necessarily. But, in fact, often yes.

Hence the time has come for reexaming the uses of utopia. Utopia is designedly mind-blowing. It aims to free the imagination. It refuses to assign immutability to structures that can change. It questions the assumptions that pragmatists take for granted. Rubem Alves, drawing on Karl Mannheim, has recently been reaffirming the importance of utopian thinking. In the Latin American context, he maintains, morality "ignores all pragmatic issues and is solely concerned with the will of God."[14] Even so, he advises "Christian realists" to read *Moral Man and Immoral Society* as well as Mannheim's *Ideology and Utopia*.

Mannheim's famous book communicates a curious ambivalence about utopia, perhaps due in part to the way in which the book was assembled from writings at different periods of Mannheim's career. Part I of the book—originally published last of all, in 1936—is basically negative toward utopia. Mannheim, obviously drawing on Marx, sees ideology as the false consciousness of dominating social groups, whose perceptions and thoughts are warped by their desire to maintain privilege. Utopia—and here he departs from Marx—is the corresponding false distortion of reality by the oppressed: "Certain oppressed groups are intellectually so strongly interested in the destruction and transformation of a given condition of society that they unwittingly see only those elements in the situation which tend to negate it. Their thinking is incapable of correctly diagnosing an existing condition of society. They are not at all concerned with what really exists; rather in their thinking they already seek to change the situation that exists.

---

[13] Ronald Stone, "The Responsibility of the Saints," *Christian Century*, vol. 90, no. 881, September 12, 1973. Similarly, William Robert Miller earlier wrote: "It was Niebuhr's influence, in fact, that caused so many seminarians to rally to the support of Martin Luther King in the name of 'Christian realism'" ("Christianity's New Morality," *New Republic*, September 3, 1966, p. 22).

[14] Rubem Alves, "Christian Realism: Ideology of the Establishment," *Christianity and Crisis*, September 17, 1973, p. 176; cf. *A Theology of Human Hope* (Washington, D.C.: Corpus Books, 1969).

Their thought is never a diagnosis of the situation; it can be used only as a direction for action." [15]

But in a later part of the book—actually published earlier, originally in 1929—Mannheim sees utopia as the mind-freeing idea whose function is "to burst the bonds of the existing order." [16] Here utopias are not simply inverse ideologies and forms of false consciousness: "But they are not ideologies, i.e. they are not ideologies in the measure and in so far as they succeed through counteractivity in transforming the existing historical reality into one more in accord with their own conceptions." [17] Often they are the realities of tomorrow. [18]

Utopianism, thus understood, may perform a highly valuable social function, and a theological ethic might encourage utopianism. But the two problems in utopianism are not eliminated. First, some utopianism, because it lacks a sense of reality, may be ineffectual and may actually impede social changes that rise out of a stronger sense of reality. Thus, Rubem Alves, after encouraging his students to utopian thinking, was heard to comment about them: "They're so utopian—in the bad sense." [19] Second, another style of utopianism indulges the strain of dogmatic intolerance that tramples on others for the sake of an imaginary good. That is, we are back to the problems Niebuhr saw in soft and hard utopianism.

Against both he set his doctrine of human nature with its warnings against expectations of perfect societies uncorrupted and unthreatened by sin. He did not, like Mannheim in 1936, emphasize equally the distortions of reality by the powerful and the oppressed; instead, he invoked the biblical bias for the poor and saw the oppressed as in a better position to unmask the frauds of society than the privileged. But he thought that no person or class was immune from sin and the false understanding that it engenders.

The frequent question today is whether ethics can appropriate Niebuhr's doctrine of sin without settling for the mediocre, without ignominious compromises. Paul Abrecht, secretary for church and society of the World Council of Churches, has reviewed the issue, using the British economist, John Maynard Keynes, as an example.

[15] Karl Mannheim, *Ideology and Utopia*, trans. Louis Wirth and Edward Shils (New York: Harcourt Brace, 1936), p. 40.

[16] Ibid., p. 193.

[17] Ibid., pp. 195–96.

[18] Ibid., p. 203.

[19] For a more theoretical statement of this theme, see Rubem Alves, "Magic and Theory," *Christianity and Crisis*, May 31, 1971, pp. 110–11.

Abrecht quotes Keynes's reminiscences of his own youth: "In short, we repudiated all versions of the doctrine of original sin, of there being insane and irrational springs of wickedness in most men. We were not aware that civilization was a thin and precarious crust erected by the personality and the will of a very few, and only maintained by rules and conventions skillfully put across and guilefully preserved. . . . The rationality which we attribute to it [human nature] led to a superficiality, not only of judgement, but also of feeling." Abrecht adds his own comment: "Keynes did not use 'sin' to justify the status quo. It seems rather to have increased his realism in knowing how and where to initiate social change." [20]

The radical utopian, of course, can reply that men like Keynes simply help to modify and perpetuate an old order that should be wiped out. The more pragmatic ethicist might answer that one volume of Keynes has done more to change industrial economies than many volumes of utopian literature in this century.

To return to Niebuhr, the argument will continue as to whether his criticism of utopianism modified too much his ardor for social change. On this issue Tom Derr has recently discovered an interesting bit of evidence, buried in the archives of the World Council of Churches and (so far as I know) unknown to any of the authors who had earlier written on Niebuhr. It was part of the correspondence preceding the Oxford Conference of 1937. Niebuhr was objecting to the argument of a continental theologian who was so christocentric and so hostile to any secular criteria of justice that, in Niebuhr's view, he had no social ethic. In refutation, Niebuhr wrote: "There is so little positive content in such a position for the relative problems which face every Christian in the social situation that I would prefer to work with the superficial believers in utopia rather than ally myself with a kind of theological profundity which falsifies the immediate situations." [21] Obviously

[20] Paul Abrecht, "The Revolution Beyond the Revolution," *Anticipation* 9 (October 1971): 31. *Anticipation* is a set of occasional mimeographed papers circulated by the Department of Church and Society, World Council of Churches. Abrecht quotes Keynes, *Two Memoirs* (London, 1949), pp. 99–100. It should be noted that Keynes's language is remarkably like Niebuhr's, but Niebuhr would also emphasize the ideological sin in any civilization erected and put across by "the will of a very few."

[21] Reinhold Niebuhr, letter to Hans Schönfeld, May 21, 1937, pre-Oxford correspondence in World Council of Churches Archives, Geneva. Quoted by Tom Derr, "The Political Thought of the Ecumenical Movement, 1900–1939" (Ph. D. diss., Columbia University and Union Theological Seminary, 1972), pp. 505–6. The slightly milder, published echo of this correspondence is in Niebuhr's essay, "Christian Faith and the Common Life," in Nils Ehrenström et al., *Christian Faith and the Common Life* (London: George Allen & Unwin, 1938), pp. 87–90.

utopia was not public enemy number 1 for Niebuhr. A greater enemy was a Christian orthodoxy that was socially impotent.

Following World War II, Niebuhr became more influential in public life. He was appointed an adviser to the Policy Planning Staff of the State Department, and he served as a U.S. delegate to UNESCO. It would be understandable if such experiences confirmed his pragmatism and his feeling that he was actually making a difference in public policy. During the years of the Cold War, there is little doubt, he expressed more confidence in American society than in his prior and subsequent years. Some sections of *The Irony of American History* (1952), though alert to the flaws of this society, underestimated the intransigent structures of guilt that he characteristically found in it. To those who blithely find fault in its "Cold War mentality," it might be said that in that era Stalinism was a real and present danger, and it is as foolish to forget its past reality as to let it be a present obsession.

It can also be recalled that during the Cold War, Niebuhr made some of his most astringent criticisms of American society. Arguing against the idea that America, in contrast to communist tyrannies, offered a favorable climate for Christianity, he said that "actually the freedom we boast sometimes develops into an idolatrous collective self-esteem." And he warned against "a dissipation of the Christian faith and its corruption by the mood of self-congratulation and complacency to which a rich and powerful nation is tempted, particularly when it is forced to engage in a long conflict with a foe, whose vices seem to prove our virtues." [22]

That Reinhold Niebuhr never lost his polemical power is evident in his last two contributions to *Christianity and Crisis*, painfully and awkwardly typed out, but pointed in their meaning. They were a devastating comment on White House religion ("The King's Chapel and the King's Court" [August 4, 1969]) and a critique of presidential despotism as it influenced the war in Vietnam ("The Presidency and the Irony of American History" [April 13, 1970]).

III. PROPHETIC ESCHATOLOGY AND POLITICAL ACTIVITY

The tension between the highest human aspirations and the demands of effective political activity is a perennial ethical issue. It appears in Karl Marx, who was both a utopian and the scathing critic of

[22] Reinhold Niebuhr, "'Favorable' Environments," *Messenger*, August 18, 1953, p. 6.

utopians. Contemporary Marxists divide into those (like Ernst Bloch) who maintain a messianic sense of history and those (like Adam Schaff, Leszek Kolakowski, and Milan Machovec) who maintain some skeptical or even comic detachment from historical messianism. Philosophical and theological ethics both work continuously with this tension.

Reinhold Niebuhr was not immune to the lure of romantic aspiration. He loved Don Quixote[23] and on occasion compared himself to the Spanish knight tilting at windmills.[24] But he knew well that Don Quixote came from the land of Spanish imperialism and, in later times, of General Franco. How does the political thinker live with Don Quixote and Franco, imaginative aspiration and the crudities of dictatorship, ecstatic love, and repressive power? Questions like these pervaded Niebuhr's scholarship and his incessant activity.

Prophetic eschatology became the theological concept by which Niebuhr maintained the tension between two themes, neither of which he would surrender: the requirements of political activity and the demands of Christian love. For him God and God's Kingdom were as real—though describable only in mythological language—as the world of political, economic, and military power. He could never forget either God or God's rebellious world.

So he sought to be a "realist," who acknowledged that nations, races, and economic classes do not give up privileges unless confronted with some manifestation of power. Yet he remembered a crucified Lord who gave himself in sacrificial love. And he sought to infuse the common life with a love enacting itself in justice.

Political justice, he wrote, "is achieved, not merely by destroying, but also by deflecting, beguiling and harnessing residual self-interest and by finding the greatest possible concurrence between self-interest and the general welfare."[25] But he believed that such concurrence could not be attained unless some people to some extent looked beyond self-interest to "a Divine Power, whose resources are greater than those of men, and whose suffering love can overcome the corruptions of man's achievements, without negating the significance of our striving."[26]

One eminent political thinker who saw the connection between faith

[23] Reinhold Niebuhr, *The Irony of American History* (New York: Charles Scribner's Sons, 1952), pp. 11–16, 167.

[24] Reinhold Niebuhr, "Ten Years That Shook My World," *Christian Century*, April 26, 1939, p. 542.

[25] Reinhold Niebuhr, *The Children of Light and the Children of Darkness* (New York: Charles Scribner's Sons, 1944), p. 186.

[26] Ibid., p. 190.

and politics in Niebuhr is Hans Morgenthau, who once said: "It is indicative of the very nature of American politics and of our thinking that it is not a statesman, not a practical politician, let alone a professor of political science or of philosophy, but a theologian who can claim this distinction of being the greatest living political philosopher of America." The reason, Morgenthau went on to say, is that Americans have tended "to take our political institutions for granted, to regard them as the best there could be, which need no philosophic justification or intellectual elaboration." Therefore, "It needed a man who could look at American society, as it were, from the outside—*sub specie aeternitatis*—to develop such a political philosophy; and that man, I think, is Reinhold Niebuhr." [27]

Niebuhr's response to such praise always included some skeptical amusement. But, to the extent that he appreciated it, he agreed in seeing his vocation as interpreting human politics in the perspective of one who sought the Kingdom of God.

Eschatology, then, rescues the political thinker from the mediocre pragmatism that seeks only to keep a system going with minor adjustments to meet strains. It has some of the same mind-blowing power of utopias. But it is critical of the claims that utopians make for their own programs or dreams. It is, in a sense, more radical than utopia, because it subjects both the present order and the utopian hope to a criticism derived from faith.

It has also a staying power that utopianism often lacks. Niebuhr criticized sharply claims that Christians are morally better than other people, and in his doctrine of grace he believed that God often chooses to work through outsiders rather than through the church, especially when the church became pretentious. But he did believe that there were inherent connections between faith and action. Those motivated by hope of utopia easily turn disillusioned when utopia is defeated or when it arrives and turns sour. Those motivated by trust in God and awareness of his Kingdom should have some defenses against the disintegration of enthusiasm into despair, so characteristic of political idealism in our time.

For these reasons a prophetic eschatology is more profound than projections of utopia. Yet, I venture the opinion, utopias have their uses, especially in a time (like our own) haunted with ennui, dis-

[27] Hans J. Morgenthau, "The Influence of Reinhold Niebuhr in American Political Life and Thought," in *Reinhold Niebuhr: A Prophetic Voice in Our Time*, ed. Harold R. Landon (Greenwich, Conn.: Seabury Press, 1962), p. 109.

appointment, and frustration. Utopias remind us that the enduring power of existing institutions is illusory, that things do not have to be the way they are, that different orderings of human affairs are possible. If eschatology relativizes all historical orders by bringing them under divine judgment, utopia may relativize them by pointing to possibilities of human devising and reordering life. It may awaken imaginations that have been dulled by the inertia of the status quo. The awakened imaginations will be more effective if they recognize Niebuhr's criticisms and thereby avoid the tyrannical bent of the hard utopians and the sentimentality of the soft utopians.

Ethical truth is not abstraction, to be captured in verbalisms. To the extent that it can be verbalized, it is a matter of addressing a situation with the word that needs to be said at that time. For this reason, as well as for others, the ethical wisdom of the past is never sufficient for our time. There is much that is impermanent in any past ethic. It is quite contrary to the spirit of a person like Reinhold Niebuhr to go on repeating his judgments—as though he had himself not built a career of criticizing his own past positions.

Even so, there is something comic in the blithe claims of trivial thinkers in every generation to go beyond the giants of the past, when they have not even understood the magnificence of their predecessors. So it is with many of the volatile crusaders and resisters of crusades in our time. We would be as foolish to try to live on the ethical capital accumulated by Niebuhr—or, for that matter, by Walter Rauschenbusch or Karl Barth or Martin Luther King, Jr.—as to ignore his wisdom.

Reinhold Niebuhr was the prophet of love as the impossible possibility. He was also the advocate of the kind of political activity that organizes power to confront oppressive power. His gift, which can never be simply copied or imitated but which can be resought, was to combine the art of the possible with the impossible possibility.

Niebuhr as Thinker and Doer

Kenneth W. Thompson

The vivid and more than life-sized image that many of us shared of
Reinhold Niebuhr as thinker and doer is still alive, but dimmed by
events and the passing years. As one set of problems follows another, his
manner of grappling with them seems very near, yet very far from
practice. To read him again is to rediscover how inseparably for him
philosophy and action were joined, how durable and lasting are his
insights and judgments, and how strongly his writings hold up decades
later. What sets him apart is a style and temper toward current problems
that remain unique. Whatever the problem, he either starts with a
general proposition or moves from the particular in that direction.
It is the principle or complex of principles that is important to him, not
the once-and-for-all "solution." Indeed, he could never escape the
conviction that false gods and absolutes were man's most virulent
social disease.

How quaint and far-removed he seems from every one of the dominant present-day approaches: positive thinking, problem solving, giving
the system one more chance, banning the bomb, ending the war,
black power, law and order, conquering hunger, eliminating waste,
reducing population, resolving conflict. Not that he did not strive to
solve problems or root out evil wherever he found them. Few have
labored so untiringly in political, social, and religious movements
that spanned the nation. But his theology and political philosophy
would not allow him to strut and pose as a savior of mankind. He could
not cast himself as a leader sent to eradicate evil, for he found too much
frailty in all men, including himself—although his humility was never
self-conscious or pompous, as with those who make a weapon out of
their limitations. His self-awareness was for himself, not something
he paraded in an intellectual fashion show. It was man's predicament
and man's possibilities, not Reinhold Niebuhr's, that were worthy of
articles and sermons and books.

Perhaps if he had continued in active writing down through the most recent period of theological experimentation and faddism, he would have told us what he personally saw, felt, and experienced in group sensitivity adventures, nude bathing at midnight, or in varieties of falling in love, to mention three of the preoccupations of our theological superstars. But I do not for a moment believe it. He would likely have polemicized against the narcissism of present-day culture, including theology. He had too much strength and moral and intellectual integrity to play at exhibitionism, although he was a consummate actor "for the glory of God." In the process, he came off well as our most powerful interpreter, but this was because life was a succession of dramas of the self and of history, not progress spiraling ever upward or a hopelessly inescapable descent into slime and ashes. Life and interpretation were one for him, united in an unending and unresolved drama. Coherence so often missing was communicated through his person, not in the kaleidescopic events about which he wrote. His individualism was integral, not a gossamer web of fictions and fantasies. He was troubled about man, but not about his own image or the ink he received or his identity. The unity of his thought and action was bound up with the unity he achieved in coming to terms with himself and the world, not once and for all, but daily. To assert this is not to prove it but to underscore a central thesis of this paper. It is a thesis that we shall follow through a discussion of Niebuhr as thinker and doer and the interconnections between the two.

THE TEMPTATIONS OF THEOLOGY AND THOUGHT

Niebuhr never presumed to be a systematic thinker or theologian. He spoke self-mockingly of his "bastardized theology." Critics have questioned whether there was a core to this thought. Moving from the pulpit of a contentious Detroit parish to the cockpit of social and religious controversy in the world's largest city, he lacked the time or opportunity to build a system of thought. Indeed, it would be difficult to picture Reinhold Niebuhr remaining passively in his study for any sustained period of time. Two forces in particular pulled him out into society. He was as impatient with the insufficiencies of every prevailing philosophy and system of thought as with society's stubborn resistance to change and its sanctifying of the status quo. It was impossible to remain aloof from the maelstrom, even though he early learned that the prospects of solving problems were modest at best. He entered the political arena not as political actor but thinker, with all the burdens and liabilities this position entailed. If theologians questioned how systematically he pursued theology, politicians doubted he was one of them—and they were right. His one attempt to gain political office in New York City ended in failure. He lived in two worlds, never fully at home in either. Perhaps this was why he understood them both better than they understood themselves, including their pretensions and self-deceptions, interests, and illusions.

The temptation of most thinkers and theologians is to stand above, beyond, or outside the social arena in judgment on those caught up in the bruising struggles and bewildering dilemmas of social and political life. In the first phase of Niebuhr's thought, in the 1920s and 1930s, he sought to make Christianity relevant to the pressing problems of the day. He ranged himself with those who spoke for a social gospel. His mentor was the social gospel Episcopal Bishop Charles Williams, whom he described as a lonely dissenting voice amidst the religious complacency of Detroit. He quoted with approval the bishop's words that in social justice there were only two Christians in Detroit and they were both Jews.

At this stage, he chose the prophetic for the passive role that a residual Lutheranism might have inspired. More important, he chose to do battle with Henry Ford I and the mighty leaders of the new mass-production auto industry who promised to solve all social problems but aggravated most of them. If passivity tempts the traditional theologian, the threatening presence of the influential and the powerful can intimidate the social and political thinker, the more so if he seeks to influence or gain support or share authority with those who hold power. The spider's web of the powerful ties the hands and restricts the freedom of social thinkers, especially those who would be both thinkers and doers. Intellectuals who make no pretense of influencing the powerful are immune; thoroughgoing social critics and muckrakers have no designs on decision makers, and they are not dependent upon them. But Niebuhr was one who carried his thinking into the market place. He numbered among close friends and acquaintances the powerful and the mighty in government and business, education, and the mass media. From his early days of indignation over social injustices in Detroit focusing on Henry Ford I to some rather shrill debates with Henry Luce on America's role in the world, he never flinched or counted the cost of meeting powerful leaders head on.

Perhaps we have grown too sophisticated or clever, or it may be that the price of serious criticism is greater today, conceivably because the powerful are less secure in their power than Ford or Luce. Yet it is difficult to mention anyone who plays the critic's role today which Niebuhr did in his time, while always continuing to have a modicum of influence over policymakers. Not that he endeared himself to those he criticized. I knew at least two secretaries of state who complained that they could not understand him—the classic defense against a foe whose criticism has found its target. He was as rigorous with intellectuals, including those whose ideas he respected, but they were more accustomed to intellectual rigor. Harold Laski, in a debate, once questioned how Niebuhr could be a Christian while being so unrelenting in his criticism of Christian practice. Niebuhr's answer, while totally mild, disarmed Laski: "I criticize my wife but I believe in and love her."

The ultimate temptation for thinkers, of course, is to hold back on the reins of social criticism within their own established groups. Both self-interest and ideals so dictate. By contrast, Niebuhr within the organized church was a continuing critic, for example, of the National Council of Churches. His criticism, however, was criticism with a difference. It was directed at the ideas and tendencies of man and institutions, seldom, if ever, at their intentions or motivations. And it was criticism for which Niebuhr took full responsibility, never hiding behind the collective position of a board of editors, particularly when he was most outspoken. In 1955, I wrote an article on "Prophets and Politics" which was critical of the National Council's position in international relations. To avoid any embarrassment to the foundation with which I was associated, I asked if it could be published anonymously. Niebuhr replied: "If we publish the article anonymously we [*Christianity and Crisis*] rather attack the National Council of Churches directly while if we could publish it under your name it would not be a direct attack."[1] He saw the theologian and thinker standing alone in his criticism bearing full responsibility for his dissent.

It was in the controversy over foreign policy between World Wars I and II that Niebuhr single-handedly, it seemed, challenged the prevailing view of the churches. He set out to overturn a too-simple pacifism that had spread through the Protestant churches and fostered isolationism toward the impending struggle with Hitler. His thesis was "that modern Christian and secular perfectionism, which places a premium upon non-participation in conflict, is a very sentimental

[1] Letter to author, March 22, 1955.

version of the Christian faith and is at variance with the profoundest insights of the Christian religion." [2] It ignores the fact that international politics involves rivalries and conflicts that can be resolved or mitigated not through some abstract system of justice but through an equilibrium of power. Nations, including the United States, must create counter-vailing power against the most powerful and aggressive state which seeks to dominate all the rest. He wrote: "There has never been a scheme of justice in history which did not have a balance of power at its foundation." [3]

Pacifism ignores the fact that both in the social and political order love and conformity to some of Christ's ultimate precepts are not a simple possibility. The injunctions "resist not evil" and "be not anxious for your life" are part of a total ethic that men violate not only in war time but every day of their lives. Anxiety is an inevitable concomitant of human freedom of man who is dependent upon God but seeks to make himself self-sufficient and independent. The rivalries among nations are played out in personal life, Niebuhr writes, as when "my little five-year-old boy comes to me with the tale of an attack made upon him by his year-old sister. This tale is concocted to escape parental judgment for being too rough in playing with his sister. One is reminded of Germany's claim that Poland was the aggressor and the similar Russian charge against Finland." [4]

Pacifists "assert that if only men loved one another, all the complex and sometimes horrible realities of the political order could be dispensed with." [5] Their "if" begs the central question of human history. "It is because men are sinners that justice can be achieved only by a certain degree of coercion on the one hand, and by a resistance to coercion and tyranny on the other hand." [6] By saying that peaceful nations need not resist tyranny, pacifists show a preference not for good but for evil. History proves them wrong when they assert that tyranny will fall of its own inner decay. They are also wrong in saying that all governments are oppressive and therefore the tyranny in Nazi Germany was no worse than that of the so-called democratic states. In a statement which foreshadows his stress on relative moral discrimination throughout the rest of his career, Niebuhr proclaimed: "Whatever may be the moral ambiguities of the so-called democratic nations, and however

[2] *Christianity and Power Politics* (New York: Charles Scribner's Sons, 1946), p. ix.
[3] Ibid., p. 104.
[4] Ibid., p. 14.
[5] Ibid.
[6] Ibid.

serious may be their failure to conform perfectly to their democratic ideals, it is sheer moral perversity to equate the inconsistencies of a democratic civilization with the brutalities which modern tyrannical states practise. If we cannot make a distinction here, there are no historical distinctions which have any value."[7] He concluded that every distinction on which the fate of civilizations has turned has been this kind of relative dictinction.

Niebuhr turned the resulting international political order that pacifist policies would bring about against them. He refused to allow them to postulate a condition of perfect peace as their alternative to an order in which power was organized against nations who sought overwhelming power. He described a system in which such power would go unchallenged as "peace, but . . . a peace which has nothing to do with the Kingdom of God. It is a peace which results from one will establishing a complete dominion over other wills and reducing them to acquiescence."[8]

Thus, by arguing his case both on moral and political grounds and staking out the principles and guidelines he was to elaborate, apply, and refine over more than three decades, Niebuhr swept isolationism before him and laid the groundwork for Christian realism. Long before American political scientists made fashionable the idea of system-building or structures of thought, Niebuhr's thinking evolved into a more-or-less coherent pattern of viewing political problems. It was an open structure, however, for he remained skeptical of rigid and rationalistic modes and approaches, which he was persuaded did not fit historical reality. To systembuilding in the social sciences he proposed as an alternative the historical sciences, which remained open to the intrusion of empirical data. However much he qualified and whatever his caveats, Niebuhr did evolve a theory of ethics and politics that provided the basis for serious intellectual dialogue both with ethicists (whom he criticized for being too utopian) and political realists (who were too cynical). More important, this theory enabled him to criticize the powerful and mighty and to do it within an organized framework of thought.

He went so far as to say that the man of power was always to a certain degree an anti-Christ. He quoted Lord Acton and observed that if the men of power were to take this absolutely seriously, they would lose their power. It is probably well, since power is inevitable

[7] Ibid., pp. 15–16.
[8] Ibid., p. 16.

in the world, that men of conscience rather than scoundrels should use it. "But if men of power had not only conscience but also something of the gospel's insight into the intricacies of social sin in the world, they would know that they could never extricate themselves completely from the sinfulness of power, even while they were wielding it ostensibly for the common good." [9]

Because he spoke in theological terms and the language of political thought, Niebuhr was freer to offer moral judgments of individuals and movements. His strictures on others were no different from his self-judgment, and the point he kept making was that a man's virtue and Christian commitments in no way freed him from the abuses of power. "Cromwell," he wrote, "really wanted to do the will of God—and thought he was doing it. Yet nothing in Cromwell's religion could save his dictatorship from being abortive and self-devouring." [10]

Powerful men, he once wrote, "had better be admonished that after they have done what they think right they will still remain unprofitable servants." [11] For anyone who has exercised power and pondered the moral implications, the lesson is clear. It may be offensive, particularly for those who in their lifetime have done immense good, but the gravest risk in any culture is that the strong will listen only to sycophants.

THE TEMPTATIONS OF THE DOERS

Niebuhr was, of course, no less a doer than a thinker. He was willing as political actor to subject himself and his friends to the same forms of criticism he voiced against "outsiders." Indeed, the most significant characteristic of Niebuhr's criticism is the fact it was self-criticism and was leveled against those closest to him at some time or another in his intellectual journey: liberals and intellectuals, church leaders and moralists, theologians and philosophers, sometime socialists and ideologues, pragmatists and political realists. There had to be weight and significance either intellectually or politically for someone to be his target. Because self-criticism involved dialogue with himself, he saw the same process in effect with others.

Niebuhr, therefore, was nearly immune to the most virulent disease which can seize the doer, self-deception and self-delusion. Because he

9 Ibid., p. 163.
10 Ibid., pp. 163–64.
11 Ibid., p. 165.

understood politics and society well, he had no illusions when he entered politics. Moreover, his self-awareness guarded him from the moral self-righteousness that sweeps over those who are comparatively realistic, at least in theory, before they enter the political fray. I remember complaining to Niebuhr in the 1950s about the attitudes of delegates to an annual meeting of the Americans for Democratic Action (ADA) who one day applauded men like Senator Hubert Humphrey and the next turned on them with frenzied self-righteousness—and this long before Vietnam. Niebuhr smiled wryly and said this was something he and Elmer Davis, the radio commentator, had had to counter from the beginnings of ADA.

But the sense of moral superiority of doers runs deeper than that. They are driven by their anxiety and insecurity to claim more for themselves than they deserve or intend. Niebuhr talked of this situation in one context as the security-power dilemma. Men and nations seek power to assure their independence and security, but the margin of their power is never enough to guarantee absolute security. Hence, the struggle for power spirals upward and men are caught in a tragic dilemma. What they undertook for the limited end of assuring their own safety and survival expands of its own momentum. They turn to moral claims and pretensions to justify what becomes for others a threat to their security. And once the conflict is seen in absolute moral terms, the prospects for conflict resolution critically diminish. Then political rivals become crusaders and political warfare takes on all the characteristics of a holy war.

Niebuhr gave the question of individual and national self-righteousness in politics the highest priority. It was perhaps the single most recurrent theme in his writing on politics. But he was also aware of the terrible predicament of the doer caught up in the throes of decision making. Especially in the later realistic phase of his work, he expressed sympathy for the hard-pressed policymaker hemmed in by conflicting interests, pursued by the hounds of time, and driven by pride and ambition. During much of the lifetime of Franklin D. Roosevelt, Niebuhr had criticized his policies, though not his foreign policy. He ranged himself with those on the left who considered that Roosevelt had compromised too often and too early with those on the right, abandoning thereby genuine programs of social reform. As time passed, Niebuhr, given what June Bingham has called "the courage to change," was increasingly persuaded that it was Roosevelt who saved the United States from a major upheaval and even bloody revolution through the reforms of a moderately progressive administration. It was Roosevelt's policies that enabled America to refute the Marxist prophecy. Similarly, he was impressed by the capacity of President Harry S. Truman to make decisions and was generally supportive of his foreign policy. It may be that he was more closely in touch with leaders here and in subsequent administrations and therefore more attuned to their thinking. However, a more likely explanation for his greater sympathy was a keener awareness of the narrowing effects on choice of the constraints of leadership. Incidentally, Niebuhr, far from being an apologist for national administrations, remained an ever-vigilant critic. But he also took issue with those who denounced national leaders without taking into account the heavy burdens and restrictive context within which policies were formulated and carried out.

If Niebuhr was concerned with any single occupational hazard of the decision maker, it was the inevitable immediacy of his concerns and his short-term horizon. Leaders were responsible to national and local constituencies, he wrote, and must defend and give voice to such interests. Policymakers seldom, if ever, could rise above the national interest. But the people were capable of better than this. They were freer to think in broader terms transcending the national interest. In this sense, the public could give national leaders the grounds for transcending the national interest. Both he and John Bennett quoted Robert Kennedy who urged churchmen to push the administration to go further in pursuing moral ends. They had in mind religious and humanitarian organizations in which a concerned public could organize and concert its influence. Yet Niebuhr to the end of his life remained skeptical of utopian thinkers who pretended that the possibilities of transcending the national interest were greater than they were. He was impatient not only with policymakers who viewed the world through too narrow lenses, but also with moralists who looked down from their towering heights and judged those who were struggling to bring about a tolerable measure of social justice. The moralist or humanist begins "by protesting against orthodox Christianity's bringing 'Christ down from above'; it ends by seeking to 'bring Christ up from the dead.'"[12] In other words, the moralist constructs a Christ out of some human goal or virtue. What condemns both policymakers and moralists alike is their corruptibility at the point of their greatest strength and success. In Niebuhr's words: "Trust no man.

[12] *Beyond Tragedy* (New York: Charles Scribner's Sons, 1955), p. 245.

Every man has his own capacities but also his own weaknesses. Every historic group in society has its own unique contribution to make. But there is no form of human goodness which cannot be and will not be corrupted, particularly in the day of its success." [13]

It is striking that Niebuhr found in the common man or "man in the street" a measure of common sense that was often lacking in the policymaker and the moralist. Thus he observed: "The wisdom of the man in the street never fails to comprehend the mixture of creativity and self-concern in the behavior of all his fellows. This is the achievement of a genuine non-academic 'empiricism.'" [14] Common sense takes human egotism and self-interest for granted at all levels in human relations but reacts with "gentle or harsh cynicism to it according to its degree [and] its vexatiousness. . . ." [15] It is not that the common man is more virtuous or wise. Nor are the poor or the young or the intelligent more trustworthy than the rich or the old or the ignorant. In a remarkable essay, "The Ultimate Trust," written in the mid-1950s, he asked if there was any single group men could trust; this essay anticipates so much of the debate and experience of the 1960s. To the poor whom Marxists and Christians alike see as redeemers of mankind, Niebuhr was willing to assign at most a provisional trust, although he acknowledged there was merit in recognizing their needs. However, "if the poor man is generally trusted as a social force of high destiny in society he will achieve the power to overturn society and build a new social order. . . . The prophets who lead him in the wilderness will become the priest-kings of the new order . . . [and] the one prophet who has gained all the power will kill his fellow prophets." [16] Niebuhr pointed to Stalin and his persecution of his enemies, but one could find at least as many contemporary examples, not only in totalitarian countries. He therefore concludes: "Only a person who allows unconscious utopian illusions to be transmuted into conscious lies will be able to view such contemporary facts without admitting that a too unqualified trust in the poor man as redeemer will be the very force by which the poor man becomes untrustworthy." [17]

Niebuhr also refers to the belief in youth and the movements that

[13] Ibid., pp. 130–31.
[14] *The Self and the Dramas of History* (New York: Charles Scribner's Sons, 1955), p. 135.
[15] Ibid.
[16] *Beyond Tragedy*, p. 130.
[17] Ibid.

grew up following World War I, and once more his insights have relevance for the 1960s. He notes what was obvious then and in our times—that youth brings heroism, fresh conscience, and self-sacrifice, while the old are "habituated to ancient vices."[18] The world needs the vitality and hope with which each new generation approaches age-old problems. "But it is significant that all these youth movements of Europe have in this latter day been captured by the various nationalistic hysterias of the Continent; . . . the most fanatic disciples of fanatic religion are young people. . . . Human pride has taken just another form."[19]

In the same way the poor and the young are corrupted by influence and power, intellectuals or thinkers, and policymakers or doers fall prey to hubris. But for Niebuhr it is more than hubris; it is an inevitable and inescapable stage in their journey and a temptation from which none is immune.

TRANSCENDING TEMPTATION THROUGH THOUGHT AND ACTION

Niebuhr, from his days in Detroit to his postretirement service, sought to combine thinking and doing. It is possible to explain this attempt by arguing that his intellectual and physical vitality preordained it. But this explanation is not fully satisfying because Niebuhr continued in both worlds even when his physical powers were in decline. A more likely explanation is that consciously or instinctively he sensed that he might be able to transcend the tendencies inherent in one world by living likewise in the other. Pure thought or full-time action might have made him as arrogant and self-righteous as many about whom he wrote. Or if he had remained on the periphery of one or the other realm, rather than moving toward its center, the effects of the other world might never have been felt. Because he knew both worlds well, he could speak of them with sympathy and authority and point to the human risks they carried for those who chose them. In this he is probably unique, and his outlook on man and society can be understood if we remember him as equally thinker and doer.

[18] Ibid., p. 127.
[19] Ibid., pp. 127–28.

A Selected Bibliography

The definitive checklist of Reinhold Niebuhr's writings in the period between 1916 and 1954 is to be found in *Reinhold Niebuhr's Works: A Bibliography*, by D. B. Robertson (Berea, Ky.: Berea College Press, 1954). This bibliography was reissued in *Reinhold Niebuhr: His Religious, Social, and Political Thought*, ed. Charles W. Kegley and Robert W. Bretall (New York: Macmillan Co., 1956); and, for this edition, Professor Robertson extended his checklist through the year 1955.

PRINCIPAL WORKS OF REINHOLD NIEBUHR

Does Civilization Need Religion?—A Study in the Social Resources and Limitations of Religion in Modern Life. New York: Macmillan Co., 1927.

Leaves from the Notebook of a Tamed Cynic. Chicago: Willett, Clark & Colby, 1929.

The Contribution of Religion to Social Work. New York: Columbia University Press, 1932.

Moral Man and Immoral Society: A Study in Ethics and Politics. New York: Charles Scribner's Sons, 1932.

Reflections on the End of an Era. New York: Charles Scribner's Sons, 1934.

An Interpretation of Christian Ethics. New York: Harper & Bros., 1935.

Beyond Tragedy: Essays on the Christian Interpretation of History. New York: Charles Scribner's Sons, 1937.

Christianity and Power Politics. New York: Charles Scribner's Sons, 1940.

The Nature and Destiny of Man: A Christian Interpretation. Vol. 1, *Human Nature.* New York: Charles Scribner's Sons, 1941. Vol. 2, *Human Destiny.* New York: Charles Scribner's Sons, 1943.

The Children of Light and the Children of Darkness: A Vindication of Democracy and a Critique of Its Traditional Defence. New York: Charles Scribner's Sons, 1944.

Discerning the Signs of the Times: Sermons for Today and Tomorrow. New York: Charles Scribner's Sons, 1946.

Faith and History: A Comparison of Christian and Modern Views of History. New York: Charles Scribner's Sons, 1949.

The Irony of American History. New York: Charles Scribner's Sons, 1952.

Christian Realism and Political Problems. New York: Charles Scribner's Sons, 1953.

The Self and the Dramas of History. New York: Charles Scribner's Sons, 1955.

Love and Justice. Edited by D. B. Robertson. Philadelphia: Westminster Press, 1957.

The World Crisis and American Responsibility. Edited by Ernest W. Lefever. New York: Association Press, 1958.

The Godly and the Ungodly: Essays on the Religious and Secular Dimensions of Modern Life. London: Faber & Faber, 1958.

Pious and Secular America. New York: Charles Scribner's Sons, 1958.

Essays in Applied Christianity. Edited by D. B. Robertson. New York: World Publishing Co., Meridian Books, 1959.

The Structure of Nations and Empires: A Study of the Recurring Patterns and Problems of the Political Order in Relation to the Unique Problems of the Nuclear Age. New York: Charles Scribner's Sons, 1959.

A Selected Bibliography

Reinhold Niebuhr on Politics. Edited by Harry R. Davis and Robert C. Good. New
York: Charles Scribner's Sons, 1960.

*A Nation So Conceived: Reflections on the History of America from Its Early Visions to Its
Present Power.* With Alan Heimert. New York: Charles Scribner's Sons, 1963.

Man's Nature and His Communities. New York: Charles Scribner's Sons, 1965.

*Faith and Politics: A Commentary on Religious, Social, and Political Thought in a
Technological Age.* Edited by Ronald H. Stone. New York: George Braziller,
Inc., 1968.

The Democratic Experience: Past and Prospects. With Paul E. Sigmund. New York:
Frederick A. Praeger, Inc., 1969.

Justice and Mercy. Edited by Ursula M. Niebuhr. New York: Harper & Row, 1974.

CRITICAL AND BIOGRAPHICAL STUDIES

Bingham, June. *Courage to Change: An Introduction to the Life and Thought of
Reinhold Niebuhr.* New York: Charles Scribner's Sons, 1961.

Davies, D. R. *Reinhold Niebuhr: Prophet from America.* London: James Clarke Co.,
1945.

Fackre, Gabriel J. *The Promise of Reinhold Niebuhr.* Philadelphia: J. B. Lippincott
Co., 1970.

Harland, Gordon. *The Thought of Reinhold Niebuhr.* New York: Oxford University
Press, 1960.

Hofmann, Hans. *The Theology of Reinhold Niebuhr.* Translated by Louise Pet-
tibone Smith. New York: Charles Scribner's Sons, 1956.

Kegley, Charles W., and Robert W. Bretall, eds. *Reinhold Niebuhr: His Religious,
Social, and Political Thought.* Vol. 2. Library of Living Theology. New York:
Macmillan Co., 1956.

Landon, Harold R., ed. *Reinhold Niebuhr: A Prophetic Voice in Our Time.* Greenwich, Conn.: Seabury Press, 1962.

Scott, Nathan A., Jr. *Reinhold Niebuhr.* Pamphlets on American Writers, no. 31.
Minneapolis: University of Minnesota Press, 1963. Reissued in *Makers of
American Thought: An Introduction to Seven American Writers,* edited by Ralph
Ross. Minneapolis: University of Minnesota Press, 1974.

Stone, Ronald H. *Reinhold Niebuhr: Prophet to Politicians.* Nashville, Tenn.:
Abingdon Press, 1972.

Vignaux, Georgette P. *La théologie de l'histoire chez Reinhold Niebuhr.* Neuchâtel:
Delachaux & Niestlé, 1957.

Notes on Contributors

NATHAN A. SCOTT, JR., is Shailer Mathews Professor of Theology and Literature at the University of Chicago. Among his numerous books are *The Broken Center: Studies in the Theological Horizon of Modern Literature* (1966), *Negative Capability: Studies in the New Literature and the Religious Situation* (1969), *The Wild Prayer of Longing: Poetry and the Sacred* (1971), and *Three American Moralists—Mailer, Bellow, Trilling* (1973).

ROBERT McAFEE BROWN is professor of religious studies at Stanford University. His recent writings include *The Pseudonyms of God* (1972), *Frontiers for the Church Today* (1973), *Religion and Violence* (1973), and *Is Faith Obsolete?* (1974). He is at present working on a collection of writings in the field of liberation theology and doing research on the theme of "theology as narrative."

MARTIN E. MARTY is professor of the history of the modern Christianity in the Divinity School of the University of Chicago and associate dean of the Divinity School. He is the author of numerous books and articles on religion in American history and culture, including *Righteous Empire* for which he received the National Book Award in 1973.

LANGDON GILKEY is professor of Christian theology in the Divinity School of the University of Chicago. Among his numerous books are *Maker of Heaven and Earth* (1959), *Naming the Whirlwind: The Renewal of God-Language* (1969), and *Religion and the Scientific Future* (1970).

FRANKLIN I. GAMWELL is assistant professor of religion at Manhattanville College in Purchase, New York. He received his Ph.D. degree in 1973 from the Divinity School of the University of Chicago and devoted his doctoral dissertation to Reinhold Niebuhr.

ROGER L. SHINN is Reinhold Niebuhr Professor of Social Ethics at Union Theological Seminary and adjunct professor of religion at Columbia University. His most recent book is *Wars and Rumors of Wars* (1973).

KENNETH W. THOMPSON is presently directing a study of Higher Education for Development, sponsored by a group of major international,

national, and private assistance agencies under the auspices of the International Council for Educational Development. He was previously vice-president of the Rockefeller Foundation. He has written extensively on international relations and ethics. His most recent book is *Foreign Assistance: A View from the Private Sector* (1973).

Index

Index

Burial rites, 21
Bushnell, Horace, 9, 30

Calvinism, 16, 25, 60
Camus, Albert, 88
Capitalism, 18, 36, 91
Catholicism: and development of public theology, 8, 34; the role of
   Christ in, 39
Chardin, Teilhard de, 86
"Children of light and of darkness" (Niebuhr's), 63, 64, 86
Christ: and anti-Christ, 105; and anti-pragmatism, 91; and eschatology,
   39; in moralist's view, 108; in Niebuhr's thought, 37, 41n, 43, 52; and
   pacifism, 104; as a symbol of sacrificial love, 67, 82
Christian Century, 11, 20, 29, 30
Christianity: American, 12, 96; function of, 37, 97; moral superiority of,
   98; Niebuhr as critic of, 103, 104, 108; and orthodoxy, 96; and the
   poor, 109; and realism, 105
Christianity and Crisis (Niebuhr), 29, 96, 103
Christianity and Society (Niebuhr), 88
Christianity and the Social Crisis (Rauschenbusch), 9
Christianizing the Social Order (Rauschenbusch), 9
Christian Nurture (Bushnell), 9
Christian theism, 65, 67
Church: black, 8, 22, 23, 34; definition of, 17; denominations in, 21–23;
   and the middle class, 24, 25; segregation in, 34
"Civil religion," 35
Class behavior, 22–30, 94
Classical idealism, 64
Classicism: history and meaning of, 64–66, 77, 82–84; and sacrificial love
   and perfect harmony, 69
Coffin, Henry Sloane, 4
Common sense, 20, 109
Communism, 36, 88. *See also* Marxism, Stalinism
Comte, Auguste, 13
Conservatism, 92
Corruption, 69; and Christianity, 99; and Divine Power, 97; and politics,
   87; and power, 110, and utopia, 94
Courage to Change, The (Bingham), 17
Covenant, 42
Cox, Harvey, 86
Criticism, Niebuhr's view of, 4, 5, 18, 103, 106, 107
Cromwell, Oliver, 106

Darwinism, 25

Index

Freedom, 52–56, 76n; within American Christianity, 96; and anxiety, 104; and harmony, 66, 80; self-transcendent, 73, 79; and social structures, 45, 46
Freudianism, 19
Fulfillment, historical, 75–77, 80, 81
Fundamentalism, 27
Funerals, 21
Future: and man's ontological structure, 45, 46; in vertical and temporal dialectics, 40–44

Gamwell, Franklin I., 63–84
Gilkey, Langdon, 36–62
God: and Christianity, 98; doctrine of, 66, 82; realness of, 97; in vertical and temporal dialectics, 39–44, 50–54, 61
Goodness, 67
Gospel, 37, 49, 50–52, 60, 61
Government, 49
Grace: freedom through, 55, 56; and the Reformation, 59, 87; sanctification through, 47–50, 61; and sin, 88; and utopianism, 98
Graham, Billy, 89
Guilt, 56, 57, 87, 96

Hamilton, William, 86
Harmony, perfect, 66–69, 70n, 72–80
Hecker, Father Issac, 8
Hegel, Georg Wilhelm Friedrich, 16
Heimann, Eduard, 91, 92
Heimert, Alan, 31
History, 6, 36–62; meaning in, transcendence of, 65–76; and pragmatism, 92, and public theology development, 8–10; and secularism, 64, 65; tyranny in, 104; utopianism in, 88
History of the Work of Redemption (Edwards), 9
Hitler, Adolph, 29, 103
Hope, 42, 44, 51, 55
"Human Destiny" (Niebuhr), 4
Humanist, 108
"Human Nature" (Niebuhr), 4
Humphrey, Hubert, 92, 107

Idealism, 20, 64, 88
"Idealist and Realist Political Theories" (Niebuhr), 87
Ideology, 25, 92
Ideology and Utopia (Mannheim), 93, 94
Idolatry, 26, 31, 32, 65, 96, 100

118

Index

Index